# *The Black Dog Wags Its Tail:*

## *How to deal with depression.*

# by Keith Fuller



*Published in Timaru, New Zealand, by the author using CreateSpace*

*jeanlucpublishing@gmail.com*

**Second edition published July 2018.**

# Contents.

For Nicole

## 1.      Depression: What is it?

We all have ups and downs. We all experience good moods and bad moods. This is nothing neither new nor revelatory. At most times in our lives there is a predominance of good mood. Things can still go wrong but we generally take them in our stride. We acknowledge our own goodness (self-worth, self esteem, moral character, call it what you will) and we acknowledge the goodness of the majority of people. We generally have a positive, if realistic, view of life. We accept this as usual. It is important to acknowledge this right at the start.

Why do we need to acknowledge this? Because in our Judeo-Christian heritage (and in other philosophies of other societies, such as the Confucianism of the Chinese thinker Xunzi (c. 312-230 BCE)) the natural state of humanity is regarded as evil and some intervention is required to restore the nature of humanity to that which it enjoyed in some previous golden age. This is the basic doctrine of the Christian Church, the same church which for millennia was dominant in our Western societal tradition.

And it is wrong.

Consequently, I am suggesting that we pause, take a

breath and, no matter how good or bad we feel at the moment, take time to acknowledge that life is good and that the vast majority of people are good.

Retired New Zealand homicide detective Rod Drew remains 'optimistic about humanity' even after a working life spent dealing with the worst of humanity, noting that there are few 'evil people' in the world.[1]

The New Zealand poet Brian Turner says in the introduction to his book *Boundaries,* 'It's (referencing the book, and, ergo, life) about trying to ensure that satisfaction, gratification, contentment, happiness, generosity, care and compassion and fair play and so on get the better of, and prevail over, their converse more often than not.'[2]

And, by and large, that is what happens. It is better to have lived than not to have lived.

We must also acknowledge that life is never good all of the time. Experience and common sense tell us that. We need to experience bad things in life in order to put into proper context the good things we also experience. To put it another way, it is hard to know what sweet is unless you

---

[1] http://www.stuff.co.nz/national/crime/80132822/decades-investigating-darkest-crimes-does-not-dent-top-detectives-optimism. Accessed 24/05/2016.
[2] Turner, Brian: (2015). *Boundaries.* New Zealand. Penguin Random House p.12

have tasted sour.

But at times life seems more bad than good. Everything just seems to go wrong. We say things like 'today was a total waste of makeup' and 'one step forward and two backward' and we retreat into an environment where we feel more in control: on the couch in our pyjamas or potting about in our sheds or wherever. These times may last longer than one day. We can have days of incessant trips to the doctors, work hassles or car hassles but we hunker down and endure, mindful that things will eventually get better and we will feel better about ourselves and our situation.

Two things are worthy of note in regard to our negative experiences. Firstly, they are not examples of major depression. They are just part of the ups and downs of life. Secondly, the strategies we use to deal with these negative experiences, retreat, endure and hope, can be used to help us deal with depression.

So what is depression? Think about all the ups and downs of life, the rollercoaster ride of everyday existence and the longer, perhaps more eventful, road trip of life. Now take out all the ups, leaving only the downs. All of the ups. Not some, or most but all of them. There are only the downs left. Nothing positive remains. Everything is negative, all of the time. Your experience of life now suggests life is totally bad, that there is nothing good to be experienced in life or about life, about your life or even about you. This feeling, this negativity simply will not go away. It is there when you wake up in the morning, it hangs around you all day like a bad smell you just cannot get rid of and it is with you last thing at night when you are trying to get to sleep. If you do manage to get to sleep it may even haunt your dreams. This goes on day after day after day. The negativity is overwhelming. This is depression. Welcome to my world.

Ellen Nott describes it like this. 'I was floating alone in a cold, dark and silent ocean, watching life on the shore go on like it always had. I felt remote, removed. The early days of anguish and crying gave way to a feeling of utter emptiness, where everything but the sound of my own thoughts was muted. Every awful thing I'd thought about myself, or thought others had thought about me, played on a Greatest Hits CD in my head that I couldn't turn off.'[3]

The clinicians term this major depression or clinical depression. There is, as we shall see, a particular set of

---

[3] http://www.stuff.co.nz/life-style/wellbeing/7868558/How-not-to-talk-about-depression; accessed 19/05/2013.

clinical parameters that describe major depression or clinical depression or whatever the currently fashionable term is. When I talk about depression it is this major, or clinical, depression I am referring to.

An analogy I like to use is that depression is like a black hole, of the cosmological variety.

A black hole forms when a massive star burns itself out. It literally runs out of fuel. We all know that hot gases expand, and the burning star expands outwards, constrained only by the gravity pushing inwards. The bigger the star, the greater the expansion and therefore the greater the gravity due to the greater mass of the star. The outwards expansion of the burning star is balanced by the inwards push of gravity, and while this balance holds the star can burn away happily for millions, even billions of years. But when it runs out of fuel there is nothing to balance the inward push of gravity and the star collapses in on itself. If the star is big enough, it forms a black hole. (Our sun is not big enough to form a black hole when it burns out, but the same mechanism will apply. It is just that the end result will be a neutron star or a dwarf star rather than a black hole.)

Here is the first bit of the analogy. Major depression is

often the result of burn out and feels like your whole world is collapsing in on itself. The gravity of depression literally pulls you in on yourself (pushing in if seen from the outside). Your world collapses around you and you withdraw deeper and deeper into yourself.

Here is the second bit of the analogy. A person suffering from depression sucks everything into themselves, just as a black hole does. They take, from anything, anywhere, anyone. That is why it can be hard work being around someone who is suffering from major depression. This is part of the illness. The depressed person does not have the inclination, the energy or even feels the obligation to acknowledge the humanity of others, to participate in a two way relationship or to see things from another's perspective. They have withdrawn into themselves, shutting out the outside world and, consequently, those in it. The depressed person may not want to shut everyone out but has little choice. For them, it is simply a survival strategy. They are doing what they need to do to survive, which, after all, is what any of us would do.

But here, in the third part of the analogy, is the kicker, so to say. 'Black holes ain't so black.'[4] It was originally

---

[4] The title of Chapter 7 of Stephen Hawking's 1988 book '*A Brief History of Time*', published by Bantam Press, London.

thought that nothing could escape the gravitational pull of a black hole, such was the immensity of its gravity. But Hawking has showed this is not the case. 'Things can get out of a black hole, both to the outside, and possibly, to another universe. So, if you feel you are in a black hole, don't give up. There's a way out.'[5]

Time for a short dabble in the 'official' psychological stuff.

The 'official' psychological stuff I am referencing is contained in the DSM-IV-TR (The Diagnostic System of the American Psychiatric Association) as reported in Davison, Gerald C.; Neale, John M.; Kring, Anne M. (2004). *Abnormal Psychology* (Ninth Edition). Hoboken, NJ: John Wiley & Sons, pages 269-270. This basically says that you suffer from major depression (sometimes called clinical depression) if you have depressed mood and loss of interest and pleasure for at least two weeks, *and* four of the following: difficulties in sleeping, shift in activity level (becoming either lethargic or agitated), poor appetite and weight loss or increased appetite and weight gain, loss of energy or great fatigue, negative self-concept (feelings of worthlessness and guilt), difficulty in concentrating and recurrent thoughts of death or suicide.

---

[5] Stephen Hawking: '*Into a Black Hole*'. http://www.hawking.org.uk/into-a-black-hole.html retrieved 16 July 2018.

I can only cite my own experience of these symptoms as an example. I had depressed mood and a loss of interest in usual activities, leading to an inability to find anything pleasurable (like the things I usually took pleasure in, such as cycling and walking along the seafront). I was not sleeping to the point where I was exhausted from lack of sleep. I dreaded going to bed because I knew I would toss and turn all night while waiting for the dawn to come. I became very lethargic, so much so that someone observing me would see that I was moving very slowly in everything I did, even in simple things like walking down to the mailbox to check the mail. I lost my appetite to the point where I had to force myself to eat because, rationally, I knew I had to eat to stay alive, but emotionally I felt I did not deserve the food I was consuming. An enormous fatigue seemed to settle on me and impacted everything I tried to do. It was like walking through clinging knee deep mud. I felt I was a failure, utterly worthless and that anything and everything I had done or tried to do would and had turned to custard. I simply did not deserve to carry on living and consuming the resources necessary to live and became convinced that I, and the world, would be better off if I were dead. I knew that if I drove the car into the garage, closed the door of the garage and left the engine running, no-one would notice. It would work.

This is major depression. It is not the 'I am feeling stressed/everything seems to be getting on top of me/I can't cope/please give me some happy pills' depressed mood that people experience from time to time. Doctors do dole out anti-depressants (by the truckload, it seems) for depressed mood (especially in Western societies), but I repeat: this is not major depression. People who suffer from major depression resent this trivialization of depression.

Major depression is no fun. It is also very hard to fake. The level of negativity involved in major depression is virtually incomprehensible to someone (including those who treat people suffering from major depression) who has not themselves experienced it.

Is that it? to borrow the title of Bob Geldof's autobiography. No. There is more. There is something called dysthymic disorder or simply dysthymia. This sounds really bad because it has an impressive sounding name which is of Neo Latin origin. Etymologically speaking the word is from Greek and simply means a 'bad (dys) mental disorder (thymia)'. Simply put it refers to a less severe but longer lasting form of depression. It could be characterized as chronic minor depression. One of the best illustrations of dysthymia is, for me, found in A. A. Milne's fictional character of Eeyore, the chronically depressed donkey who lived(s) in the Hundred Acre Wood. A. A. Milne's different characters may, intentionally, represent different facets of human character, what I would call human being. Eeyore is one of my favourite characters and a pencil drawing I once did of him sits on my grandson's tallboy.

Clinically speaking dysthymia is regarded as a less severe form of depression because it requires the presence of only three of the symptoms of depression listed above, not the five required for major depression. However these symptoms must be present for at least two months, compared to the two week duration required for major depression. Because it is chronic and unrelenting, often lasting for years or even a lifetime, it is questionable whether it is less severe for the patient. The symptoms may be less severe but this lesser severity is more than compensated for by the duration of the symptoms. At least one longitudinal study (a study which follows a group of patients for a long time) (Klein, et al., 2000 as quoted in Davison et al., 2004, pg 272) suggests that patients with dysthymia were more likely to try to kill themselves and had more 'impairments in functioning' than patients with major depression. My own experience is that I found, in middle age, that I had suffered from dysthymia since childhood, and because of my childhood. (It took a few years of serious navel gazing to unpack this, even though I report it in a fleeting sentence or two.) I grew up thinking my negative environment, my negative outlook on life, my 'self' if you like, were all perfectly normal, simply because as a child I did not know any better. The 'abused' child grows up thinking the abuse is normal. Psychological abuse, as I have found, can be just as damaging as physical abuse.

So there is major depression and there is dysthymia. Major depression can be episodic, while dysthymia operates a little more quietly, but continuously, in the background. This distinction is somewhat artificial, but it serves to illustrate the essential difference between the two. It is also important to note that terms like 'major depression' and 'dysthymia' are descriptors of what happens to people rather than being definitive terms with clear cut boundaries.

I have alluded to my experience of major depression. I have also alluded to my experience of dysthymia. Yes, you can have both at the same time. This is sometimes referred to as double depression, although this term doesn't seem to have caught on among clinicians in New

Zealand yet. It is common, in my experience anyway, for your family doctor to think in terms of one or the other. To be fair to family doctors they have ten to fifteen minutes to sort out a problem that may have been months or even years in the making, and they rely heavily on what the depressive patient tells them about their depression. Some people are better at communicating how they feel than others, and depression, by its very nature, makes communication with others difficult. So I do not want to be down on family doctors, however I do want to call it like I see it, and as I said, the way I see it doctors tend to think in terms of one or the other, rather than both.

I also think it is wrong to say that one recovers from an episode of major depression in the same way one recovers from a bout of the flu. In the midst of an episode of flu one often yearns for the time when one did not have the flu, so pervasive is the discomfort from it. Although it may be difficult to accept at the time, the flu will pass and there will again be a time when we do not have the flu. The flu has gone, and we get on with our lives as usual. I do not think the same can be said for depression. Major depression takes us to a very dark place and while we may come back from that place we cannot ever forget our experience of that place. The simple fact is that we have been there and the simple realization is that we may go there again. Once the genie is out of the bottle, it can never be fully put back in. We are forever changed by the experience. In my view every episode of major depression weakens the self. Eventually the difference between major depression and dysthymia blurs and we have what I would call chronic major depression. This is my situation. It is, from my perspective, a very fragile situation.

I have suggested that having depression is like perceiving that there are no ups, only downs in life. The depressed person perceives everything as negative. Does that mean that there are no ups, only downs? No. That is what the depressed person *perceives*. That perception is a reality for the depressed person. Yet it is hardly ever the reality other people perceive. And reality can change. Therein lies a therapeutic opportunity.

Let me tell you a story to illustrate what I mean, or more accurately several different versions of the same story. In this story a woman crosses the road. (I never said it was going to be an exciting story.)

In the first version of this story a woman wants to cross the road (to get to the other side; I mean, why else?). She stands at the kerb, looks right, then left and then right again and then, *perceiving* the way to be clear and that there are no cars coming, sets off across the road and makes it safely to the other side. End of story.

Now in the second version, a woman wants to cross the road. She looks right, then left, then right again and *perceives* that there are no cars coming. She sets off across the road and is hit by an oncoming car and killed.

What is the same in this version of the story and the first version of the story and what is different?

What is the same is that she *perceives* there are no cars coming, just as she did in the first version of this story. What is different is that this time there *are* cars coming. The unfortunate woman *perceived* there were no cars coming when in fact there were. *But she acted on her perception.* We all act on what we perceive to be, which may or may not be what actually is. (This opens up a whole line of philosophical thought about our existence. Do we exist, or do we simply *perceive* that we exist? How can we exist in order that we *perceive* our existence? What is the nature of our existence? Are we, in fact, lying motionless in some alternate reality while sensory perceptions are fed to our brain to make it *seem* we exist? (This is the basic thesis of The Matrix trilogy.) This interesting intellectual conundrum has occupied the mind of many a philosopher but let's not go there.)

This realization can not only help us to see how the depressed person views their situation but also opens up a therapeutic opportunity. This is illustrated by the third version of the story.

The woman is now part of a group of women who wish to cross the road. They all stand at the kerb, look both ways, and then the woman sets off across the road. Suddenly two arms reach out, one on either side of her, each taking hold of her and stopping her from crossing the road. 'There's a car coming,' says one of the other women. 'Oh, my goodness, I didn't see it!' exclaims the woman as she is assaulted by the realization of what might have happened if the other women had not stopped her in her tracks.

Once again she acted on her *perception*. Once again her perception was different from what actually *was*. But this time her friends noticed the discrepancy between her perception and what was actually happening and *intervened* to stop her acting on her perception.

When the depressed person's perception gets out of kilter with 'reality' (in the common sense of the word, rather than the philosophical sense) other people may see this and be able to intervene to correct it. It is not quite as simple as stopping someone crossing the road but the principle is the same.

A word here about suicide (and yes, I have come *very* close to it). Depression often leads to suicide as we all know. But it is my view that the depressed person does not *want* to be dead. It is just that the depressed person *perceives* no other way out of their situation. That does not mean there *is* no way out of their situation. (If you are of a philosophical bent you may choose to notice the importance of the verb *'to be'* in all this.) It simply means that the depressed person cannot comprehend that there is a way out, or what that way out might be. Someone else may well be able to see one or both of these things.

In any situation, there is always a way through, a course of action that is best to follow, a way to sensibly deal with stuff. It may not be immediately clear *what* that way is. Simply knowing that there is a way through is sufficient. It is also necessary. (Again, philosophers will recognize the importance of something being both necessary and sufficient.)

This means that someone other than the depressed person can look at the depressed person's situation and, seeing it differently, can reassure the depressed person that there is a way through. It is okay if the depressed person and even the observer cannot see *what* that way is. But it is necessary and sufficient for the depressed person to simply accept that there is a way through, an alternative to suicide.

Another word, this time about reality. (Philosophers love to talk about reality and can and do at (often) tedious length. I shall endeavour to restrain my verbosity.) I have drawn a distinction between the life (perceptions) of the depressed person and the lives (perceptions) of other people, or of life outside of the depressed person. This is proper but a word of caution is needed. The beginnings of this caution are noted in the realization that we *all* act on our perceptions. We all act on what we perceive to be and we hope that what we perceive is in fact in close accordance with what others perceive to be. In other words, all life is subjective.

Why is this important? We need to be aware that there is no one objective view of reality. There is no one right way to see things. The best we can do is accept that our way of looking at things is mostly the same as someone else's way of looking at things. But only we have our view of the world, our perception of the world. Everyone else's is slightly different, depending on their viewpoint. This helps us retain our individuality in the midst of a community of people of fairly similar perceptions.

We also need to be aware that there are people (and institutions) who are all too ready to tell us that reality is objective, not subjective. They and they alone know the nature of this objective reality (and of course if you join them and give them all your money they will share this esoteric knowledge with you!). Sound familiar? Probably because you don't have to look too far around a liberal Western society before you see an example of what I mean. This church has the answer. But so does the one down the road. And the one across town. This political ideology is the answer. But so is the one propagated by the proponents of this other political ideology. Do you see how ludicrous such claims are? Incidentally, it is the curse of the tolerant that they tolerate even the intolerant. That is why there are so many competing claims of objective reality in a liberal society.

What specific objective realities are we talking about? Plato's Theory of Forms is one example. His 'perfect realm' where the perfect form of anything can be found is entirely objective. The monotheistic god of Judaism, Christianity and Islam is another. (I am not setting out to put a downer on religion here, which even the death of God philosopher Frederick Nietzsche admitted adds value to human life; I am simply calling it like I see it.) The idea of the mechanistic unchangeable universe championed by Issac Newton is another. These and other so-called objective realities do not exist. The same goes for the tooth fairy and Father Christmas. (I myself was particularly devastated about the tooth fairy. At my age, if they come out, they don't grow back!) The closest we come to any sort of objective reality in the twenty-first century is the speed of light which, according to Einstein, nothing can go faster than.

Why is it necessary to make this point in a book about depression? Because like our experience of any 'abnormality' we seek to return to a place of 'normality'; we want to be like everyone else, to counter our subjective low mood with a good dose of objective reality. But thinking like this is delusional. All our realities are subjective. It is true that our subjective realities overlap to a very large extent. If this were not so, we would not be able to function in this world. We have a functional need to look at an object and see (mostly) the same thing that other people see. But no one else can see the object *exactly* as we see it because they cannot look at it through our eyes. Neither is there a perfect form of the object available to be seen. We can *only* look at the object through our eyes. Likewise life is only visible to us as we see it. Our life *is* our reality. The depressed person's depression is real to them. That is their reality. We cannot say to them 'Oh it's all in your head; you're imagining it – just get over it!' To hear that is simply devastating to a depressed person.

One of the effects of depression is to convince the depressed person that they are the only person who feels like this and that everybody else is 'normal' and 'happy' and 'well-adjusted'. They long to be like all the other people they see in the shopping mall, all the other 'well' people who do not have hang-ups or concerns. They have fallen out of what they think is an objective reality and long to be part of it once more. They want something that is simply not there. It is a delusion, a mirage on the horizon of everyday life.

This realization can help the depressed person go from fighting the depression (pretending I don't have depression) to managing the depression (living with it).

How? This helps in two ways.

Firstly, the depressed person comes to realize they are not

alone. Other people also suffer from depression, and, lo and behold, life goes on. The depression becomes manageable. You don't have to 'cure' it in order to rejoin human society. Depressed people are part of society and that is okay.

Secondly, the unrealistic expectation of an objective reality, especially one devoid of depression, is removed. Suddenly the burden is not so heavy and the journey's goal not so far away.

So that is depression. What I have described is not an exhaustive analysis of what depression is like, but rather what it is like for me and for one or two others who have written about it. My intent is to paint a picture of depression that realistically portrays it as it is. If one concludes from this portrayal that depression is nasty, life sapping and soul destroying then I have done my job. Depression destroys lives. But all is not complete and utter hopelessness, even if it may seem that way. The picture I have painted of depression indicates aspects of the depressed person's reality which can be used to treat and manage depression. These we shall explore.

## 2.        What does it do to you?

The devastation caused by depression is, I think, often underestimated. It is a debilitating illness. The effects of depression are often compounded by becoming the causes of worsening the depression. Isolation is one example of this.

Depression isolates you from family, from society and even from yourself. This is because depression is a withdrawing into oneself, a journey into the darkest reaches of our mind. It is a journey the depressed person must make on his or her own. It is thus a lonely journey. It is a journey the depressed person would in all likelihood rather not make, but by now the luxury of choice has long been removed from script. The feeling of dread that is invoked by the realization of the inevitably of going on this journey simply compounds the depression.

The aloneness, and the loneliness, lead inevitably to isolation. Being among people is no consolation. As Gerry Rafferty sang in *Baker Street*, in reference to London, 'This city desert makes you feel so cold. It's got so many people but it's got no soul.'[6]

Because the depressed person withdraws from contact

---

[6] http://www.azlyrics.com/lyrics/gerryrafferty/bakerstreet.html

with others, withdraws simply to be in a place that feels safe, withdraws simply as a means of self-preservation, the depressed person becomes more depressed, simply as a result of the withdrawal. This is a common feature of depression. Effect becomes cause which then becomes effect which then becomes cause and on and on it goes. This is why people talk about spiraling down into depression. It goes round and round and down and down until either you can break free of this vicious spiral or you kill yourself.

Co-incident with this withdrawal is a shutting down of the normal functions of a human being. Any contact with other human beings is entirely superficial. Here we must state what to be some will be obvious. The depressed person is very good at masking their depression, even to themselves. The depressed person may not seem to you to be depressed. That does not mean they are not.

When considering whether a person is depressed one must consider the context of the human being, your prior knowledge of the human being and what that human being is communicating to you non-verbally. Reliance on one at the expense of the others is dangerous. An agreement of all three assessments is usually necessary to confirm depression. What the person is telling you may be the most unreliable of the information presented.

Depression dominates your view of your self and of life. It is like looking at everything through blackened lenses. Even the things the depressed person may have previously enjoyed, favourite hobbies or activities or movies or books or people, will no longer hold any joy for the depressed person. Depression is all pervasive. It contaminates, pollutes, everything it comes into contact with, every aspect of the depressed person's life. Nothing, and I mean no thing, is enjoyable anymore, regardless of how enjoyable it may have once been.

Depression can encourage you to beat yourself up in public in order to find (search, beg for, crave) reassurance to the contrary. In other words, you may try to cope with your depression by employing self-deprecating humour (as I did), secretly hoping that others will disagree with you and so vicariously reinforce your self-worth. Unfortunately this does not always happen. As Eleanor Catton wrote in her Man Booker prize-winning novel *'The Luminaries'* (2013; Victoria University Press, Wellington) '...deprecation always waits to be disputed, and, if the disputation does not come, becomes petulance.' (p. 56).

Depression lowers your resilience. You are not able to take things in your stride anymore. The slightest little thing can shatter your ability to cope. One example which I find has this effect on me is encountering aggressive driving. The driving does not necessarily have to directly affect me. Simply witnessing such driving, thereby being violently reminded of the presence of aggressive people in our society, is sufficient to pull the rug out from under me.

Depression changes people's perception of you. You may seem to them withdrawn, preoccupied, as if you do not want to be with others, to speak with others. You are indeed preoccupied, usually with trying to cope with the situation, which you do by withdrawing from it to lessen your interaction with the situation and those involved in it. Hence you are perceived by others as moody, as aloof, so that they will not want to make the extra effort required to engage you in any meaningful conversation or other social intercourse. Then you will think that no-one cares, no-one can be bothered with you which invariably will have the effect of making your depression worse. Again we see the downward spiral where effect becomes cause which then becomes a worse effect.

The irony is that in this depressed place you crave human interaction at the same time as you are consciously or unconsciously pushing other people away from you. This is because the withdrawal and aloofness is a survival mechanism. You are withdrawing into a safe place, into the sanctity of your cave as it were. That is the only place you feel safe. You want to talk to people, you want to be with people, but your primary need is to feel safe and you can only do that, in your mind, by withdrawing, which causes people to shun you. This downwards spiral is one of the most dangerous features of depression. It is analogous to the onset of hypothermia. The symptoms of hypothermia, lethargy and withdrawal, actively act against the person recognizing, and treating, their hypothermia, thereby allowing their hypothermia to get worse. Depression operates in much the same way.

Depression can make you angry. Anger is, by its nature, directed at someone, even some thing, and usually for some reason, real or imagined. We can usually measure the degree of justification of our anger by comparing it with the cause of the anger, at least the cause that we perceive. Often our anger is out of proportion to its proximate cause, such as when a child breaks a plate or someone makes a mistake in front of us while we are driving. Once the irrational expression of anger surfaces a rational moderation of the emotion dominates and our anger is seen in its proper perspective. Depression takes away the moderating influence of perspective. Our anger can spontaneously erupt over often little things. What is worse is that we know, perhaps intuitively, that our anger is way out of proportion to its cause but we just cannot help ourselves. Then we beat ourselves up for getting angry, even while we are still angry. Sometimes our anger is latent, bubbling away quietly beneath the surface but surreptitiously sabotaging our mood, stealthily creeping into our consciousness but at the same time cleverly disguising not only its very presence but its root cause.

Here we have a situation where a person is not only not aware of the cause of their anger but is not aware of the anger itself, nor of the negative affect it has on the person and on their interpersonal relationships. This is not a sustainable situation – it cannot endure. But it can last for years, particularly if the person is intellectually able, to some extent at least, to override the anger. Sooner or later, though, it will erupt, directed either outward to the world or inward to the person. Sometimes, perhaps often, the person, or the clinicians the person seeks help from, work at dealing with the eruption but not the cause of the eruption. The result is of course predictable. This treatment or methodology, call it what you will, only postpones the inevitable re-eruption and the person finds themselves in a cycle of crash and burn and recover until someone or something brings the person to their senses and the person addresses the cause of the repeated eruptions. Often that something is an episode that brings the person very close to losing it all. That is what depression does do to you. It is not pretty, no matter which way you look at it.

This leads us to a further consideration. Even an eruption of anger can seem to the depressed person as 'doing the right thing', such is the persuasive nature of depression in masking its destructiveness. Consequently your judgment is adversely affected.

Depression negatively affects your ability to make decisions. You are looking at things through darkened lenses as it were and so you make decisions based solely on what you see, not on what is actually there. Inevitably these are bad decisions. In desperation you want to trust people and so you pin all your hopes on others, but time and time again your trust is, in your view, betrayed, because you are asking of others something they simply cannot give. You realize the futility of this and turn your back on others, withdrawing into your own world, trusting no-one. To trust no-one is to go to a very lonely place. To protect yourself from this hurt repeating itself you reason that it is better to be in a lonely place trusting no-one than to be hurt again. You lurch back and forth between these two extremes, clutching at the straws of trust you see in other people and then withdrawing inward because the straws crumple in your grip and you cannot stand to be hurt again. You just want a way out this. Any way will do. Anything that you think gives you a way out becomes a possibility. Gradually, as this possibility goes around and around in your head you invest it with inevitability, infallibility, and the bad decision is born.

Depression damages relationships. This may seem obvious. No-one wants to be around a sad sack all the time. Your lack of energy, of motivation and of anything resembling initiative or spark simply is not propitious of constructive human intercourse. You are too hard to deal with, you demand too much and give back too little. It all becomes too one-sided. This is very destructive.

Firstly, you do not realize you are doing it. Apathy seems normal to you while 'making an effort' seems abnormal.

Secondly, and similarly, you are not aware of the negativity you exude. In a room full of people you seem able to drag everyone else down to your level of mood, down to a lowest common denominator determined by where you are at.

Thirdly, it is too much to ask other people in a relationship with you to constantly base that relationship on how you are feeling, on what's going on for you. From the point of view of the other person your negativity is negating their being, their sense of self, their sense of who they are as a sentient thinking being. This was brought home to me by my faithful Labrador Misty (now deceased). For all her devotion and loyalty to her master, her friendship and her doggy way of understanding, there were times when she simply did not want to be with me because my mood was so low. She would go off into a little clearing among some trees and not come out for hours. This of course made me feel guilty for letting my depression affect her in this way, which, naturally, worsened my depression. Again the downward spiral. When the other being in a relationship is a human being, with his or her own sense of self, dreams, plans, hopes and desires, how much harder must it be for that being to put aside all sense of self, every dream, every plan, every hope and every desire, simply because you cannot respond to it, cannot cope with it, simply because you do not wish to know.

Fourthly, there is the guilt visited upon the other person. Is this person depressed because of something I have done, or have not done, because of something I am or something I am not, because of some aspect of my being, because of me? Why can I not help this person? Nothing I seem to do has any effect, does any good.

This all sounds rather negative, as if all there is to do if you are in a relationship with a depressed person is to leave, bail out, look after yourself. For some people, and in some situations, things may well come to that. But there are other less destructive strategies available to cope with being in a relationship with a depressed person. These are the responsibility of both people in the relationship. They are talked about later, in the more constructive part of the book, but to help point you to them they involve the depressed person taking responsibility for his or her health and for the other person in the relationship to accept that depression is part of the depressed person's being, that is, to simply accept the depressed person for who they are.

## 3.    What causes it?

We need, I think, to acknowledge that causality in a general sense is not as straightforward as either we might like or we might expect. We are all both the cause and the effect of each others existence. In our context this means that there is much about your identity as a person, the nature of your being, that is determined long before you become capable of significant self–reflection. This determination has its genesis both in your genetic inheritance and in your formative environment. (The Dunedin Multidisciplinary Health and Development Research Unit (commonly known as *'The Dunedin Study')* affirms the importance of both genetic inheritance (nature) and formative environment (nurture) in the determination of your being, as reported in the acclaimed television documentary series *'Why Am I?'* which screened on Television One in New Zealand in 2016.) Such a determination is virtually absolute at birth and falls away as you approach adult life and accumulate life experience. Depression may be part of that determination.

Depression may also result from traumatic life experience as an adult. Here we need to recognize that while different people can react to different things differently, it is also true, as a consequence of the variety of our human being, that different people can react to the *same* things differently. Thus we need to exercise caution in gauging the severity of our reaction to some traumatic event against the severity of someone else's reaction to the same or to a similar event. Simply because this person coped with (insert whatever traumatic event is relevant) without experiencing depression does not mean to say that I, or someone else, will also cope with (insert the same traumatic event as above) without experiencing depression, and perhaps more to the point, it does not mean to say that I or someone else *should* cope with (traumatic event) without experiencing depression. As Elvis Presley wrote and sang, 'Before you abuse, criticize and accuse, walk a mile in my shoes.'[7]

A traumatic life experience may also trigger latent depression that has lingered in the background since your formative years. For example, as a result of your childhood environment you may have suffered a mild form of depression for most of your life (dysthymia) without realizing it simply because to you the way you felt was normal. Then, later in life you suffer an unrelated discrete traumatic event which, while other healthy people who

---

[7] http://www.azlyrics.com/lyrics/elvispresley/walkamileinmyshoes.html

suffer the same event get through without experiencing depression, pushes you over the edge (a tipping point) from which there is no return and you are faced with the inevitability of having to deal with your depression or leave it to deal (rather unkindly) with you. If the traumatic life event is severe (for example, nursing soldiers during a war; witnessing repeated atrocities) this may in itself be sufficient (but not necessary) to trigger major depression.

Depression may also be without apparent cause. The mere fact that you exist is to you somewhat depressing. You see life as pointless and nothing but a struggle. It is all 'just a waste of time'[8]. Some people call this existential depression. It is, I think, important to recognize the genetic disposition to depression that is rampant in some family lines. Given the stigma associated with depression until quite recently (and even still associated with it) your ancestors may not have admitted to depression, and, or, your ancestor's family may have hidden the depression, and even the depressed person, from the inquiring gaze of history and genealogy. Nothing of course can be done about your ancestors. So if there is a genetic tendency toward depression in your family, you are stuck with it. If this

---

[8] From the lyrics of 'Mother' by Roger Waters and sung by Pink Floyd. http://www.azlyrics.com/lyrics/pinkfloyd/mother.html

sounds unfair we must remember we all have genetic tendencies toward this and that, some are good and some are not so good.

The other part to this is that not only do you inherit stuff from your ancestors, but simply because they are *your* ancestors you tend to grow up with them. To put it another way, the very ancestors from whom you may have inherited a genetic tendency toward depression (in most cases, a parent) are also responsible for you during your formative years. Your most formative years are from birth to around seven or eight years old. During that time a lot of behavioural and attitudinal aspects are fixed. If the dominant parent in the family (one parent is always dominant, often, in Western families, the mother) is also the depressive parent, then not only do you inherit the tendency toward depression but you are significantly influenced by that depressive parent, sometimes, even often, to the extent that your formative environment imbues in you a lot of negativity.

There is little you can do about that. By the time you reach an age when you not only realize what has been happening but are in a position to do something about it, the damage is already done.

There is a hint here at a theme I wish to develop at some

length in this work. It is this. The genetic disposition toward depression is internal to you. It has to do with the way you see the world. The influence of a dominant, depressed parent is external to you. It has to do with the environment you are in, in this case, the environment you are growing up in. Depression, as an illness of the mind, is always a result of things both internal and external to you. It is also not a matter of simply classifying some thing as 'external' or 'internal'. What is internal and what is external take part in a dynamic interchange. One influences the other and round and round it goes. This of course is true not only for depression. It is the way our mind (consciousness, being, call it what you will, but I refer to that part of ourselves which is more than simply the physical self, that is, the metaphysical self) works and is shaped by what happens to us. It continues all our lives. Our life is a constant stream of sensing what is happening around us, analyzing that information and acting on it. That we act on that information influences the world around us. We are changing the world that is changing us. We analyze this change and then, again, act accordingly. There is a constant interplay of external and internal, each influencing the other, the sum of which forms our thinking and our actions.

Let's look at an example. Children are throwing a ball to one another. When the ball comes towards the child the child's eye senses the change in light, converts that information into electrical signals and sends it to the occipital cortex at the back of the brain (external). The occipital cortex decodes the electrical signals and creates an 'image' of the ball's flight in the child's mind (the child is 'conscious' of the ball flying through the air). It then sends a signal (or multiple signals) to the frontal cortex of the brain where a decision is made about how to respond to the incoming ball (internal). Since such a response, e.g. to catch the ball, requires that signals are then sent to the motor cortex of the brain, situated on the right side of the head. The motor cortex receives the analysis of the ball's flight path and extends an arm up to the right position in order for the hand to catch the ball (external). The outside environment is influenced by the ball either being caught or not caught. In each case the children react appropriately to the circumstances.

This interplay of internal and external things is in my opinion crucial to our understanding of our human being. Everything we think and do forms part of this dynamic.

There will be times when either the external aspect dominates or the internal aspect dominates. The younger we are the more likely the external will dominate the internal. As we grow old and grow up (which, of course, are not necessarily the same thing) the internal aspect of our minds will become stronger as we gain significant life experience. The balance between internal and external things will change throughout our lifetime, but, I will argue later, should follow a general tendency to favour the internal as we age. (There are hints here of the human being as a chaotic system, a topic I shall return to later. For now, let me just say the essence of a chaotic system is unpredictably.)

There are of course times when the influence of external things is so large that it almost overwhelms the mind's ability to analyze and respond accordingly. One obvious example, especially to the people of Canterbury in the South Island of New Zealand, is a major earthquake. We are at the 'mercy' so to speak of nature. (I don't like using the word 'mercy' here because the implication is that nature is capable of mercy, which it clearly is not. An earthquake is neither good nor evil; it is just a natural event on the planet on which we live.) We (I was there at the time) had no warning of the earthquake, there is nothing we could have done to stop the earthquake and we simply had to ride it out. We may have been disoriented for a few minutes as our minds struggle to analyze and react to the number and magnitude of external stimuli being fed into them by our senses. Only when the earthquake has abated can we begin to make a proper response to what has just happened.

Another example is childhood abuse. This is much more insidious than an earthquake. A human child is a fragile thing, physically, psychologically and intellectually. We depend on those who nurture us for a very long time, typically about one quarter of our whole lives, before we are capable of significant self-reflection. That means we depend on something external to us (the environment created by those who nurture us) not only long before we are capable of internal reflection on that environment, but also during the time we are developing the capacity to be self-aware and consequently the means of self-reflection. We are very vulnerable at this time.

When our childhood environment is abusive, when the external influences on our vulnerable lives are negative rather than positive, the effect on us is hugely negative. We grow up with this negativity and we (by default) accept our environment as normal, for the simple reason that we have nothing else to compare it to. It is not until later in our lives, when we are able to realize that what happened to us in childhood was not "normal", that we begin to recognize the effect this has had on our lives. Often the primary manifestation of this effect is depression.

Depression is insidious because it can manifest itself in your life long before you realize that there is something wrong, let alone realize what it is that is wrong. A common experience in this realization is for the adult to suddenly understand why he or she did the things he or she has done and why particular decisions and choices were made, particularly when time has revealed them to be not the best decisions or choices. We begin to realize, then accept and then deal with the fact, that the external influences of our childhood environment have had such a negative impact on our human development that we cannot help but see ourselves and the world in which we live through the dark lenses of negativity. We might become aware we are doing that, we may even learn ways to cope with that, but what we cannot do is escape it. It is built into our being; it is part of our human being.

This explains how an overwhelming external influence can lead to depression. In it is a hint of how we might deal with this situation, if this is indeed our situation. That same hint is contained in the next little bit about internal causes.

I am going to press the matter of a distinction between external and internal causes more than is possibly, even probably, warranted because I want to make a particular point. Once the point is made I shall return to a more dynamic interplay between the two.

I have said above that we all see, or perceive, the world differently, in other words that all reality is subjective. I quickly made the point that we mostly see the world as other people see it and that this huge commonality in how disparate beings perceive the same thing enables us to function as part of a society in an interactive way. This imbues a large measure of objectivity into our subjective experience of the world, an objectivity exemplified by the simple act of our driving down the road and not hitting anyone or anything, or being hit by anyone or anything.

But what if you do not see the world as others see it?

Let's look at our example of the child catching the ball again. The child's eyes sense the change in light as the ball comes towards her. The eyes send the appropriate electrical signals to the occipital cortex. But this time, instead of creating an image of the incoming ball in the child's consciousness, the brain creates an image of an incoming rock. Where did the brain get this image from? Obviously not from the incoming ball; this looks to everyone else to be a ball. The brain has substituted the image of the ball with the image of the rock which it has pulled from somewhere in its memory, perhaps from a long forgotten previous trauma in which the child was actually hit by an incoming rock, a rock that came towards the child on roughly the same relative trajectory as the ball which is coming toward the child. The brain has confused the two and presented the child with an image of reality in her consciousness which is false. The frontal cortex makes a decision based on this false information and this time the motor cortex receives different signals. This time the imperative is not to catch the ball but to get out of the way of the rock, to duck, to turn aside, to move out of the way, preferably all at the same time. The result is the child does not catch the ball and indeed is seen to actively avoid the ball.

The other children cannot of course understand why she should try to get out of the way of the ball rather than attempt to catch it. It just seems silly, incomprehensible. For the child perceiving the incoming rock the fear of being hit and being hurt is anything but silly and incomprehensible; indeed her self-preservation flight response would have kicked in to keep her safe.

After the incoming projectile has safely passed and the ball is seen by all to be lying harmlessly uncaught on the ground, a more objective perception of the experience is available to the girl. She realizes that it was not a rock, but just a ball. She realizes why she dodged it, because at that moment it was not, to her, a ball but a rock. But how is she going to explain her behaviour to the other children? This is a problem experienced by people with depression. They see things differently from other people. Because they see things differently they react, or behave, differently, in line with how they see things rather than how things actually are. This reactive behaviour may in turn trigger further negative external stimuli, most probably, in the above example, from the other children. 'Why didn't you catch the ball? Why did you run away from it? Are you scared of it?' The child, already feeling silly for dodging a ball she thought was a rock, is made to feel even worse by the other children. She withdraws further into herself to escape the children's taunts and effect becomes cause which then becomes effect and round and round and down and down she goes.

So it is hard to talk about a cause of depression, as if you simply picked up a bug from somewhere. Changed circumstances can result in depression. Depression can result in changed circumstances. Did you lose your job because you are depressed or are you depressed because you lost your job?

This external/internal dynamic is crucial, in my opinion, to understanding the nature and origins of depression. It is never simply one or the other, never just external stimuli nor just internal thoughts which lead to depression. It is always a dynamic interplay between the two.

I feel compelled to have a little moan here about doctors who think depression has but one cause, albeit different for different patients, and once the cause has been identified and the depression has been 'fixed' the patient is well again and everything is as it was before. It is hardly ever like that. The dynamic causes of depression can be complex and understanding them can be just as complex. It is in my view probable that major depression is never 'fixed' but simply managed in a way that enables the patient to have some quality of life. Sometimes I wonder if we expect too much from our doctors, or if they expect too much from themselves and their profession, or both.

Understanding depression, or in particular your depression, is the first step in dealing with it. A further step is understanding yourself and what makes you tick (or tock, or whatever floats your boat).

Some personality types are more prone to depression than

others, simply because of the nature of that personality. My type of INFJ (on the Meyers-Briggs indicator) is, apparently, particularly prone to depression. But that raises a question. Should I be depressed because (in this case) Meyers-Briggs says that I should be depressed? Or is the Meyers-Briggs indicator simply describing what already is? It is of course the latter.

There are two points to be made here. Firstly, the external environment your inchoate self found itself in almost certainly played a role in the development of your personality type. My withdrawal into myself to escape family conflict raging all around me almost certainly contributed to my high level of introversion. Those same environmental factors may have contributed to subsequent depression (as they did in my case). This simply means that the dynamic interplay of internal thought (or consciousness or whatever you wish to call it) and external stimuli is at play here, as we have already noted. It becomes difficult to separate the formative influences of personality from the causes of depression. This is quite in order, given the complexity of human consciousness.

Secondly, even given this complexity, there is some imperative to separate the depression from the personality.

This is because personality is about who you are and depression is about what happens to you, both internally and externally. It is important to note here that indicators like those of the Meyers-Briggs personality type are, as we have noted, descriptors, not definers. They describe who you are. They do not define who you are (as if your every action and response is somehow predetermined by your personality type indicator). Such descriptions are helpful providing they are used in the process of attaining a deeper understanding of the self. But depression is neither a definer nor a descriptor.

This is important to grasp because in Western society particularly, people (and especially men) are often defined by what they do. "He's a lawyer." "She's a financial consultant." If all one does is spend one's time dealing with depression then it is not difficult to be so classified: "He's a nutcase."

This is simply not the case. We are not defined by what happens to us, by what we do or what we do not do. (While these latter two often indicate, to a greater or lesser extent, who we are they do not and cannot *define* who we are.) Nor are we defined by our weight, height, athletic ability or lack thereof. These are all things which can be used to describe us, but they do not define us. Depression is neither a defining criterion nor a descriptive statement. It is an illness. That is enough, and at the same time that is all.

In this way I hope to separate the depression from the person, in a similar way to how we separate an injury from our conception of who we are. So, for example, a person with a broken wrist is not defined by that injury, and simply has to suffer it. However, even in this somewhat trivial example it is apparent that the injury can affect our sense of being. I once remarked to an acquaintance with just such an injury, noting that she was feeling a little fed up with the limitations her injury imposed on her, that 'this too shall pass', hopefully emphasizing the transient nature of the injury in comparison to the enduring nature of the self. It seems my words provided her with some comfort while her frustration provided me with a glimpse of how even a simple injury can negatively affect the self.

Yet as much as we separate such negativity from ourselves, and this is easier with a physical injury which is confined to one particular part of the body than with a mental illness, we cannot escape it entirely. With depression, which affects the very way we see the world and thus the world that we see, this is separation is harder. But also because of that it is even more important to try and separate your depression, even artificially, from your self. Only in this way can we make any useful attempt to understand our depression and where it may have come from.

What we find when we do this is that total separation is impossible because of the dynamic interplay between the self and the depression. This is analogous to the interplay between the internal self and the external world I have already mentioned. Total separation is impossible simply because there is, and there needs to be, this dynamic interplay between the two.

But some separation, and therefore identification of both and their interdependence, opens up therapeutic opportunities in both the external world (behavioural) and the internal self (cognitive). This is why therapy for depression is often 'marketed' as Cognitive-Behaviour Therapy, or CBT (or, as I like to think of it, as CBS – Common Bloody Sense!).

A word about blame. When we identify our depression as being predominantly rooted in events and influences external to us it is natural to want to blame those events and influences for our depression. We reason, not unnaturally, that were it not for those events and influences we would not be depressed. This leads quickly to a way of thinking in which our depression is 'their' fault, whoever 'they' might be. Because it is 'their' fault we of course have no responsibility for our depression because there is nothing we can do about it. If there is nothing we can do about it then it is useless making any effort to deal with our depression. We are stuck with it and things will never get better. Thus says the victim. This train of thought is particularly evident among people who have suffered some form of abuse, particularly childhood abuse. Because childhood abuse happens, obviously, in childhood and adversely affects our formative years, and thus our formative selves, its consequent effects are hard-wired into our selves. The abused child can never escape the effects of childhood abuse even when no longer a child, and so may continually blame those ill-effects on the abuser. It is always their fault.

There is of course some truth to this. Because the effects of childhood abuse are hard-wired into our selves they last a lifetime and so can negatively impact us throughout our lives. This cannot be denied and to attempt to do so only pushes the problem away out of sight, where it will still be a problem and will still adversely affect our lives at times when, often, we might least expect it. (This is the situation of the tragic character Matilda in Shira Nayman's novel,

*'The Listener'*, except that it was not child abuse that tormented her but rather her experiences as a young nurse during the Second World War.)

When we look at the other side of the coin, if it is not *their* fault we find it hard to accept that the abuse we suffered and the consequent depression we are enduring is *our* fault. Abusive adults are, by definition, adults and should know, or have known, better.

Thus it is equally difficult for us accept the blame for depression which has its genesis in other environmental, and genetic, factors beyond our control.

So whose fault is it?

We could look to Aristotle's doctrine of the mean (or, as I mischievously like to think of it, his exposition of straight forward common sense) and apportion some blame to factors external to ourselves (our genetic make-up, the environment of our formative years or life events beyond our control) and some blame to factors internal to ourselves (this is my genetic make-up and I just have to deal with it, and my personal all time favourite piece of utterly useless 'wisdom'; other people have bad stuff happen to them and they just get over it so why can't I?). In other words the way forward invariably lies somewhere between two extremes. Our task is then to identify each of these extremes and then work out the safest, most efficient and easily attained route between them. This does sound, as I have already suggested, eminently sensible.

But it is not.

It is not because whether we go with one extreme or the other or some medium course between them we are still seeking to answer the question 'Whose fault is it?' The problem is with the question, not with the answer.

Is it anybody's fault? Does it have to be anybody's fault? The answer of course is No.

Why, then, are we obsessed with finding blame?

Years and years ago I sat in a theology lecture and listened to our systematic theology professor expound on the causal history of the brick house we could see outside the window. The bricklayer put the bricks into an orderly arrangement that ended with the walls of a house existing where none had existed before. The truck driver had transported the bricks to the site. The kiln had fired the bricks. The quarry workers had excavated the raw material for the bricks. The raw material had been deposited by some geological process. And so on, all the way back to the first cause, the genesis of this brick home, which of course was the theology professor's god. And so God exists. (This, by the way, is the basic argument for God's existence in the theology of St. Thomas Aquinas, and is referred to as the teleological argument; that is, God is known by the end result of God's actions: us and our world.) I was not particularly convinced by what I saw as a somewhat simplistic argument but I kept my mouth shut. After all, I was the student and the theology professor was (supposedly) the wise and learned man, so I simply concluded there was some part of the argument I was not getting. My lack of understanding was down to me, not down to a faulty argument. (Note the lack of confidence here – something was not right, and therefore I must be to blame. Depression had sapped my self-confidence without my even being aware of it.)

The point of this little story is to demonstrate the prominent place causality has had in our world view. Our lives have been imbued with it to such an extent that whenever something goes wrong we believe someone must be to blame. This thinking has even entered our economic world view. Everybody starts on a level playing field and if you don't succeed then it must be your fault. Because it is your fault why should we, who have succeeded, help you?

The use of a divine causality in explaining what is otherwise inexplicable underlines the extent to which causality has dominated our efforts to explain our being and the world around us. If a cause for some thing could be identified (the clouds darken and it rains, e.g.) then well and good. If a cause for some thing cannot be found then that cause must be God. As more and more of our natural world is understood, including the cosmic origins of our universe, the idea of a causal God is relegated further and further from our everyday experience. (This relegation has occasioned what some seek to call the 'death of God'. Perhaps the 'death of the idea of God' is more accurate.) Whether God, or the idea of God, has died or whether God could even be considered as a primal cause in the first place is not the point of this discussion. The point is that we have been obsessed by causality ever since we first began to wonder why things happen. Often, almost certainly more often than not, this curiousity has been productive to our understanding, both of our world and ourselves. But at times it has not. For example, if illness cannot be explained then it must be caused by God. If God is good (just for the hell of it I shall throw into the mix Socrates' question to Euthyphro: Is God good because God is God or is God God because God is good?) then God must have inflicted illness on you because of something bad you have done. (Recall the story of Job, on whom God inflicted illness even though he had done nothing wrong.

This story is informative to us, but not for reasons of causality. It is instructive in our dealing with our depression.) This is why the culmination of healing stories in the Greek Scriptures invariably end with the benediction, 'Go in peace. Your sins are forgiven.'

Our modern knowledge of medicine (which is little more than about one hundred years old, despite what generations of status-seeking doctors try to tell us) renders any link between illness and moral behaviour largely redundant and questions our whole understanding of causality.

And rightly so. What has tripped us up for many years is the conviction that everything must have a cause. To phrase this in the context of our present discussion, we have been tormented by the idea that when something goes wrong someone must be to blame.

And this is wrong. The question is not whether internal or external factors, or some medium route in between, can be blamed for our depression. The question is why are we seeking someone to blame at all? It is simply not a productive route to follow.

Consequent to this conclusion is the idea that not everything has a cause. Some things just happen. Chaos theory informs us that a design does not need (mean, point to the existence of) a designer. For example, the intricate patterns made by a large flock of starlings in flight over the city of Rome are not the result of a designer dictating the design of the patterns. Each starling simply flies in a spatial relationship to the seven birds around it. When one bird executes a turn to, say, avoid a predatory larger bird, the seven starlings in a spatial relationship with the turning starling also turn; and for each of the seven starlings in that relationship there are seven other starlings in a spatial relationship which also turn, and so on, so that the turn inductively spreads throughout the whole flock. Of course, while all this is going on another starling somewhere else in the flock also turns to avoid a predator, initiating another turn which interacts with the first turn, and so on, producing the complex patterns visible in large flocks of starlings over Rome. While the observer may perceive the flock moving as one, no one starling has an overall, what we might call an objective, view of the patterns the flock makes in flight.

Applied to our own lives the idea of chaos theory suggests that sometimes shit happens, often quite unexpectedly and for no apparent reason.

Before we get terminally dejected by the idea that we are all subject to shit beyond our control, the flip side is also valid – good things also happen unexpectedly and for no apparent reason. Further, we can exert some influence on what happens. (It is important to note here the distinction between an event which occurs randomly and an event the occurrence of which we cannot predict with certainty. Random events all have an equal probability of happening whereas chaos theory tells us that non random events have a varying probability of happening, a probability that we might reasonably determine.) A simple yet profound example is smiling at someone you pass on the street. Because of your smile the person you smiled at may have smiled at someone else, may have gone out of her way to help someone else or simply had a better day. The point is the consequences of your positive action are unpredictable (or, more accurately, predictable only to a degree of probability), but they are themselves positive.

The question which must now arise is that while all of this is well and good, we cannot escape the link between depression and, say, childhood abuse. We cannot escape the idea that there is a causal link between the two.

And of course there is. But what I wish to do is distinguish between understanding what happened and blaming someone for what happened.

Childhood abuse, for example, may have been the major

causal factor in the development of our depression. But it is unproductive to blame the abuser. (In the same way it is unproductive for the character of Matilda, mentioned above, to blame the war for her neurosis, as this will simply not help her deal with it, even though the causal relationship between the war and her neurosis is clearly established.)

It is productive to understand the genesis of our depression. This can help us deal with it. We cannot deal with that which we do not understand. But note the use of the first person here. Us. We. We have to deal with our depression. Blaming, as distinct from understanding, implies by its very nature that it is all someone else's fault. Because it is all someone else's fault we assume no responsibility and therefore have no capability for dealing with it. Then, of course, it does not get dealt with. It festers away eating at our very being. It becomes a dead end, sometimes quite literally.

No-one else can deal with our depression for us. It is, after all, our depression. Consequently it is up to us to deal with it. That may seem unfair. It probably is. Unfortunately nobody said that life was fair. By the time we realize that fact as supposedly mature supposedly responsible adults we have already been affected by the unfairness of life. This is the way it is. There is not a damn thing we can do about it. Apart from accept it. That, we can do.

Everyone has a story. Put more bluntly, everyone has their own shit to deal with. Everyone. The idea that most or even some people live perfectly happy content untroubled lives just does not cut it. One does not reach the heady status of adulthood without reflecting on, and then dealing with, some sort of shit. Welcome, as they say, to the real world.

So everyone has their own shit. But we also need to be clear that depression is by its very nature in a class of its own. Equating the two is not my point. My point is, that like the shit we all have to deal with, we need to accept that our depression is just that – our depression. This leads to understanding. And understanding leads to being able - some once fashionable sociologist or psychologist might say empowered – to deal with our depression. That is our point of entry into our therapeutic reflections on depression.

I said at the beginning of this chapter that depression can occur without apparent cause. I then went on to talk about a genetic predisposition to depression. Since then I have alluded to chaos theory and the realization that not every effect can be linked to a cause. Thus spontaneous depression can result from our realization of the existential nature of life.

Existential thought was popularized during the twentieth century by the French philosophers Satre, Camus and de Beauvoir who in turn gained inspiration from other continental philosophers such as Kiekegaard, Nietzsche and Heidegger. The philosophical school which gave voice to this thought was termed, not surprisingly, existentialism. It is, I think, widely misunderstood.

Imagine walking along a cliff top. There is no convenient safety fence along the edge of the cliff. The cliff is so high that jumping off it would mean certain death. Anyone who has ever walked along such a cliff top would have, even fleetingly, given some cognizance to the consequences of going over the cliff. The close proximity of the cliff virtually guarantees such thought.

Now imagine stopping on your walk, turning to face the cliff and advancing to within a few metres of the cliff top. There are other people around, also enjoying a cliff top walk, but they are too far from you to intervene if you were to walk to the edge of the cliff and jump off. You stand there thinking about the choice you have, to jump or not to jump. You realize that at this moment in time you have complete freedom to jump, or not to jump. You may choose to do so, or may choose not to do so; is entirely up to you. No-one in the vicinity is close enough to intervene and there are no supernatural entities that are going to miraculously stop you or catch you if you do decide to jump. The freedom to choose death stares you directly in the face. It is a choice you and you alone have. It is entirely up to you.

This radical freedom is the basis of existential thought. (It is summed up in Satre's rhetorical question, 'Should I commit suicide or should I have a cup of coffee?' The point is one is absolutely free to do one or the other.) The most well known expression of existentialist thought are the lyrics of the theme song to the TV comedy M*A*S*H, *'Suicide is painless'*.

The realization that one has this radical freedom can lead to existential depression.

Essentially existential depression, sometimes referred to as existential angst, is our response to the realization that we are all alone in the world, that we have this radical freedom and that there is no overarching meaning, structure or purpose to life. It often, but certainly not always, occurs in single people who have little or no responsibilities to others. Such responsibilities by themselves provide some meaning, structure and purpose, no matter how illusory, to our individual worlds.

It should be clear that if one perceives that one's life has no meaning, structure or purpose then despair will quickly follow. To correlate our thought with language already used, the person consumed by despair can become convinced that it matters not at all whether one continues to exist or one chooses to end one's existence. This is the reality the existentialist perceives. It is I think no coincidence that existentialist thought reached prominence during and soon after the Second World War, when all through Europe moral systems and thought gave way to banal brutality and (at times) nothing seemed to be able to stop this madness.

The same understanding we have already discussed is relevant here. Note that I have used the word 'perceives' above. I have earlier noted that we all 'perceive' our reality and that what we consider to be an objective reality is simply the realization that our perceptions are in line with other people's perceptions. Existentialism as a philosophical 'system' never really gained traction beyond the immediate influence of the Second World War. But it is true that individuals still get caught up in existentialist thought which seems to them to render their lives meaningless and of no concern to others. This can be a genesis of depression. Dealing with the resultant depression therefore involves an understanding of its genesis in existentialist thought.

No matter what we might think the genesis of our depression is, our depression is real to us. Belittling depression simply compounds the depression for the depressed person. Accepting and understanding the reality of the depression to the depressed person, both by the depressed person and by those close to the depressed person, is the first significant therapeutic step.

## 4.    Who is responsible for dealing with your depression?

The answer to this question is actually quite simple. It may have profound implications for the depressed person and for those around the depressed person but the answer remains quite simple. It has also been previously alluded to.

You are.

You, as the depressed person, are responsible for dealing with your depression. Not your doctor, nor your psychiatrist, nor your psychologist, nor your counsellor, nor your partner, nor your mother, nor your father, nor your son, nor your daughter, nor anyone else.

You are. It is your problem and you have to deal with it.

In fact, you are the only person who can deal with it. No-one else can. No-one else can see inside your head or feel what you are feeling or experience what you are experiencing. Only you have the insight, the determination and the wherewithal to deal with your depression.

There is one very good reason for this.

It has to do with human *being*.

That is what you are. A being who is human. We can discuss and debate what it means to be a human being in some detail but that more properly belongs in the realm of philosophy (which, if you haven't already figured it out, I love). Suffice it to say that the basis for our apportioning of responsibility for the treatment and management of our depression to ourselves is that we recognize each human being as a unique being. Further, Martin Heidegger, a twentieth century German philosopher who was concerned with the nature of being for the human, postulated the need for the human being to be responsible for its own existence as an indicator of that being's authenticity. (Yes I know Heidegger was a paid up member of the Nazi Party before and during the Second World War, some say because of his wish to advance his career in the German university system. No-one said that philosophers were perfect. They are merely philosophers. Before they were philosophers they were (and remained) human beings and we all know how fallible human beings are.) (I am indebted to the character of Cuthbert in Shira Nayman's previously mentioned novel who advised the director of the psychiatric hospital where the novel is set to deal with one patient by 'carry(ing) a big Heidegger'.)

All this may come as quite a shock to the system. We are not used to assuming such a level of responsibility for our own welfare, our own being, especially if we have grown up in the liberal welfare states of the twentieth century.

As we grow up our parents (hopefully) provide the necessities of life we need. We go to school and learn to conform to what is expected of us at our age. We behave according to deep seated social norms, even before we realize, or are capable of realizing, our conformity to these norms. Even if we reject these norms we often do so in conformity with others. All gang members look the same to the public. The patch, the black Harley, the black helmet and on and on it goes.

I am not suggesting this is bad. Neither am I suggesting that it is good. It simply is. (There's that verb 'to be' again.) One of the reasons for this (here I am invoking reason in an evolutionary sense) is that we all grow up needing to identify with this group or that group, with people like us. I am quite sure an evolutionary psychologist would say it is a survival thing. To ensure our survival, and the survival of our group, we tend to stick with like – minded people, be they gangs or the middle class V-neck pullover Volvo crowd so assaulted by the comedy wit of Billy Connolly.

We grow up in this way, learning the values and traditions of our group.

If we reject that group it is likely that we simply learn the values and traditions of another group, a group that we think is more suited to our own being. We are, after all, social animals.

Yet for all our need for social intercourse we remain unique human beings, one among many. It is in this primacy of unique human being that our responsibility for dealing with our depression is found.

The paradox of depression is that the illness itself militates against the individual person's ability to deal with it. This presents difficulties.

The depressed person is disabled by depression. This is not uncommon, though it is not often stated. Depression is disabling. Specifically, in our money and consumer oriented western economies, depression can mean you cannot support yourself by working. As a woman, even in our (supposedly) enlightened times this is not so bad. As a man it is devastating. Men are valued by what they do, not who they are. Men of working age who do not work can expect to be looked down upon, regardless of the validity of the reason for their not working. Society expects working age people to, well, work. This expectation is fuelled by political rhetoric from the centre right and right wing of our political establishment. Consequently the depressed person who *can* not work rather than *will* not work finds that their disability compounds their depression.

What can be done?

If a person is unable to work then two options are open to them. The first is death. The second is to be supported by the society in which the person lives. There are no other options available.

Forget the plight of the depressed person for a moment and ask yourself what sort of society you want to live in. Your answer may be tempered by the realization that you are simply a diagnosis away from having some sort of incurable disease. Any reasonable person (and here I use the term 'reasonable' in its full philosophical sense) will choose the second option. (The first option has historically been chosen, by Nazi Germany.)

Why?

There is the obvious reason of looking after others less fortunate than I because one day I could very well become one of those 'others'. This is a little selfish but as an argument for looking after others it is a clincher. (You may know this argument in its now outdated form 'There but for the grace of God go I.')

Then there is the question of what sort of society do you want to live in. Do you want to live in a society where those that are seen not to make any contribution to society, which in Western Society means not working, are killed off?

If the answer is 'No', then you need some form of societal support for those people who cannot work. And so, on the eighth day, God created WINZ (Work and Income New Zealand, the part of the Ministry of Social Development which administers welfare payments).

Even then there are some in our society who adhere to an 'if you don't work you don't eat' policy. To be told this to your face (in my case by a member of my extended family) is particularly devastating for the depressed person. Fortunately most of New Zealand society is far more enlightened in its attitudes.

Up to now I have used the words 'work' and 'contribute to our society' virtually interchangeably, and deliberately so. It is now time to unpack their different meanings.

Common sense dictates that work is not the only way people contribute to society. Child care, home making, voluntary stuff, NGO governance, keeping an eye on your elderly or vulnerable neighbours, being polite to the checkout operators and others who can often slip beneath our personable radar, all these things and more contribute to the health and wealth of our society, regardless of who does them. Such is the general level of enlightenment in

New Zealand society at least, and I have no doubt in other societies, that it is now becoming socially acceptable for Dad to stay home and look after the kids and Mum to go to work. Such evolutionary developments are actually redefining gender and parental roles, with many men actively enjoying being house husbands and consequently becoming closely engaged with their children.

This points us away from being defined by what we do to who we are. (We note, however, that the obsession with what we do is still particularly ingrained in the male psyche, especially in smaller rural areas in New Zealand, as I think is evidenced in Brian Turner's 2015 book *Boundaries*[9]). To put it another way, our sense of being begins to triumph over what we do. To put it simply, we begin to concentrate on our 'being' rather than our 'doing'.

Now we begin to see the difference between having the flu and being depressed. It is encompassed in the participles I have just used – 'having' and 'being. If one 'has' the flu then one can presumably reach a time of not 'having' the flu. But 'being' depressed affects your, well, being, who you are, your own identity.

The primacy of being emphasized here points to a distinction being made between mind and body, or as it

---

[9] Ibid.

seems fashionable to say these days, between your consciousness and your physical self.

What we have come across is what philosophers call the consciousness – body problem. We know that your mind or your consciousness interacts with your body and thus with your physical surroundings. For example, I *think* I will take a sip of coffee. I *extend* my arm, *pick* up my coffee mug and *move* it through space and time to my mouth, deftly coordinating the movement toward my mouth with the action of my hand in tipping the mug so that the coffee goes in my mouth and not down my front. So my thinking of taking a sip of coffee, an abstract thing because one cannot empirically sense a thought, has resulted in my changing my physical surroundings in such a way as to ingest coffee.

*That* this occurs is not the problem. *How* it occurs is. Specifically, how does something abstract such as a thought influence something physical such as moving a coffee mug through space and time? The historical problem in philosophy is that these are two different *types* of things. Philosophers have known of this problem for thousands of years but seem no closer to solving it (despite any number of faintly ridiculous Dan Brown novels).

A word of caution is relevant. By distinguishing between consciousness and body there is a large temptation to distinguish between the physical world and some other non-physical reality that we currently call consciousness. By saying that these two things are two different types of things we are in fact, to some extent at least, doing exactly that. But we must remember that in any consideration of the body consciousness problem (physical reality and non-physical reality) the crux of the problem is not *that* these two realities interact but *how* they do.

The point of all this is to point out that our human being is both physical and non-physical. To put it another way, being human implies a physical reality (body) and a non-physical reality (consciousness or mind).

This is better realized when we look at the brain (metaphorically; don't go doing a Hannibal Lector). What we call the brain is a vast network of biochemical electrical circuitry. It is currently (2018) the most complex thing we know of in the entire universe. (According to Moore's Law which describes the exponential advance of computing ability, by about 2025 your new desktop computer will be a match for your brain and by about 2053 it will be a match for all human brains. Human and artificial intelligence is predicted to merge this century. This will lead to a very interesting question about what it means to be human. Eventually (by about 2120) it is thought that uploading your mind (or consciousness) to a computer will be entering mainstream life. The uploading of a human mind to a computer is the basic plot of the 2014 movie 'Transcendence' directed by Wally Pfister and starring Johnny Depp as the main character.)

We know the brain has lot to do with our consciousness. People with damaged parts of their brain will exhibit corresponding changes in consciousness and related behavioural changes.

Given that the brain is a network of electrical circuitry we can see both how that network might be replicated outside the body and the difficulty in conceiving of electrical circuitry as a significant part of our being. The thing to realize is that our consciousness is composed of the *electrical messages* moving around the physical network of our brain.

Think of it this way. A city has a network of streets. That by itself does not mean anything. Things only begin to happen when traffic flows along that network. The network of streets is our brain (a physical thing). The life that comes from the traffic flowing along that network is our consciousness.

If our consciousness can be uploaded to a computer what becomes of our human being? Is our consciousness all that our human being consists of? No. It cannot be for the same reason that traffic needs a network of streets to move along. Cars by themselves just don't cut it. Cars need roads to drive on. Further, the flow of traffic is influenced by the network of streets and at the same time the network of streets is influenced by the flow of traffic. For example, you do not see four-laned median-stripped cul-de-sacs. (This reminds us of the interaction between our internal and external worlds, the dynamic result of which is the self.)

If we apply the same logic to our consciousness we realize that our consciousness needs our brain in order to – what? have life? in order to be. We may replicate and enhance our neuro – circuitry with computers, but then the computer simply becomes the street network for our consciousness to be in. In other words, your consciousness needs a physical environment in which to be and with which to interact, be it a biochemical electrical network or a replicated computer network.

All this is well and good but what does this have to do with you being responsible for your depression?

When you have the flu your body (physical self) is afflicted.

When you have depression your consciousness is afflicted. (The reader may be aware that SSRI antidepressants help depression by making the neural connections (electrical circuitry) work more effectively. Disregarding the fact that there is now some doubt about this, the way SSRI antidepressants are thought to work is only part of the story. Yes, they make the electrical circuitry work more efficiently, but then your consciousness needs at least a little time to work out that the electrical circuitry is more efficient. It is like traffic patterns adjusting to the opening of a new road. It doesn't happen immediately. This supports the idea that in depression it is our consciousness which is afflicted. It also explains why anti-depressant medication has a lag time before it becomes effective, despite increasing the efficiency of neural transmission almost immediately.)

And that is the point. It is *your* consciousness that is afflicted and only *you* can deal with it. No-one else is as aware of your consciousness as you are and no-one else has a consciousness the same as you. Legs and arms and other bits and pieces might differ in size and shape but they are essentially the same from person to person. The same cannot be said for your consciousness. It is unique to you; it is indeed who you are. It cannot exist without a context such as the brain, but the brain (or some replicated context) is not your consciousness. Your consciousness is the traffic flowing around the neural network we call the brain.

This is why depression is so debilitating. It affects your very being.

Before we all throw our hands up in despair about our need to deal with our depression sitting very uncomfortably alongside our (very proper) feelings of helplessness and hopelessness which render us vulnerable and negatively impact our ability to deal with our depression, words of caution are relevant.

What I want, and indeed need, to say, quite emphatically, is that you cannot do it on your own. Yes, I know that seems to contradict what I just said but in fact it is a truism that, once accepted, does help us to deal with our depression. I can say with some authority that I know this to be so from my own experience of depression. And while this *seems* to contradict my assertion that only you can deal with your depression in fact it does not. The distinction I am making here is between you dealing with your depression and others *helping* you deal with your depression and supporting you *while* you deal with your depression.

For example, a therapist may assist you to deal with your depression by encouraging you to order, and then express (usually verbally), your thoughts in a way that makes sense to someone else (listening to you and feeding back to you what he or she thinks you have told him or her). The therapist may encourage you to reflect on what you have said, which is of course an expression of your thought, which in turn is a product of your consciousness. By thinking, verbalizing and reflecting you are actually dealing with your depression. The therapist provides the right context for you to do this and encourages you to do so by *listening* to you.

If I seem to be suggesting that ninety percent of psychology is about empathetic listening that is simply because it is. It is surprising how infrequently we are listened to in the normal day to day lives we lead.

We are each, as adults, responsible for our own being. That does not mean we can or even should exist in isolation. The old saying that 'No man (or woman) is an island' is an old saying for a very good reason. It is true. We are social creatures. We depend on each other simply to live day to day. I am reminded of this every time I eat meat, which is usually once a day. I like meat (wiener schnitzel is my favourite, but it has to be crumbed) but there is no way in the world I am going out to the paddock to kill and cut up a cattle beast. I get my meat, like most people, in nice little sanitized packs from the supermarket. I am dependent on others to do the killing and the cutting up and packaging for me. The same principle holds for most of what we eat, wear and use during the day. Our society is one of interdependence. We depend on others not only for our physical needs but our social and emotional needs as well. We are a very complex social animal living in a very complex society.

At the same time we are, as we have already noted, responsible for our own being. This is the philosophical discussion of the one and the many, which together with the consideration of being and becoming covers the content of much philosophical reflection.

The problem occasioned by depression is that it can isolate us from society, from the very human intercourse and interdependence that can help us deal with our depression. Again we must tread carefully. Isolation (withdrawing from a difficult situation/person/environment) is a coping mechanism which those with depression will be all too familiar with. The depressed person is particularly vulnerable to negative messages about themselves and, we must be honest, not all social interaction is actually helpful. To put it bluntly, it is simply better to avoid some people. For the depressed person, this becomes most people and can of course become *all* people.

I was reminded of this when I was in the hydrotherapy pool at the local hospital, seeking to ease the symptoms of my arthritis. The pool sessions are not private and are open to any patient suffering joint problems who has been referred to the physiotherapy department. Consequently the pool is invariably populated by older people recovering from some form of joint surgery (knees, I think, were very popular). Now when one gets to a certain age medical conditions become legitimate topics of conversation, and so it was in the pool. A group of older people were conversing (comparing, boasting) about their recent surgeries and the consequent reasons they were in the pool. Isolated from this group was a young man (I would guess in his thirties or forties, but to me that is young) who, while not exhibiting any obvious medical condition, clearly moved cautiously and carefully, not exhibiting the free movement of a healthy individual. One of the older people, one of what might be called the blue rinse brigade, moved towards him (the pool is quite small) and asked him directly what was wrong with him. This was itself a bit rude. The young man hesitated at first, clearly not wanting to say anything. The woman with the blue rinse seemed impervious to the obvious distress she occasioned by her question. Eventually he replied with just one word: 'Genetics'. The implication was that whatever his condition was it was inherited and there was little he could do about it. The older woman turned back towards her group with the rather dismissive and loudly expressed comment 'Oh we've all got that!' I had wanted to spring to the defence of the young man, who was clearly offended, and silenced, by this comment, but all I could manage was to send the woman a withering look. I was so shocked that someone could be so rude that I never went back to the pool again. I withdrew for my own sake. I simply could not handle that level of negativity.

Depressed people withdraw from society, from their normal routines, in order to protect themselves from such negativity. Such isolation can of course compound your depression. This is because it isolates the depressed person not only from negativity but also from those who might help and support the depressed person as he or she deals with their depression. The trick, of course, is to protect yourself from negativity at the same time as seeking out those who might help and support you.

This seeking out of help is how the depressed person

begins to deal with their depression. Unfortunately finding such help and support can be a matter of trial and error. Those whom we might expect to be helpful turn out not to be, while help and support may come from unexpected sources, indeed its advent may even surprise us. But one thing is sure; whatever situation you find yourself in, it will change. If we are patient it will change for the better. The trick is to encourage that positive change.

How do we do that?

## 5.      How do you deal with your depression?

Okay, so it is your depression, you are responsible for dealing with it; how do you do this?

You can *treat* your depression and you can *manage* your depression. They mean quite different things (after all, they are different words) but it is likely that you will do both. What we *do* to treat and what we *do* to manage tend to be the same. The difference lies in what is accomplished by that *doing*.

I use the word 'treat' in the sense of doing things to ameliorate your depression. There are things you can do to, as far as possible, minimize it or even make it go away, though in a lot of instances this latter goal is unrealistic (despite the current thinking to the contrary in some mental health circles).

I use the word 'manage' to talk about 'living' with your depression. By this I mean 'coping' with it, living with it in a way that the impact of your depression on your daily life is minimized.

There is an easy way to clearly distinguish between treating your depression and managing it. In the first your depression goes away or is minimized and you feel better. This is about your depression. In the second your depression does not go away but it is not such a big deal anymore. This is about you and your attitude to your depression.

The proportion in which you do one or the other is unique to you. There is no magic formula that is able to tell you how much you should treat your depression and how much you should manage it, despite what some medical professionals may tell you. The importance of managing your depression is however a nod to the often chronic nature of depression.

It is important to note here that while treating your depression with a view to it going away has an obvious aim and an obvious marker for success (you no longer have depression), the aim and the marker for success in managing your depression is not nearly so obvious. Indeed talk of managing your depression may even seem like giving up, yielding to it, as if to say 'I just cannot be bothered anymore.' This is not so. The aim for managing your depression is that you are in control of your depression, rather than it being in control of you. The marker for success in managing your depression is then affirmation of this control.

One of the rather more insidious aspects of depression is that the very you that is seeking to treat and manage your depression is also the very you that is depressed. The self that is afflicted by a chronic condition is trying to treat and manage that same self's sense of wellness. It is rather like trying to lift yourself off the ground. I know from experience that at times it can seem just as futile. However the very nature of the treatment and management of depression indicates a separation of the self and the depression. This provides a therapeutic opportunity.

The first thing to do when confronting depression is admit that you have depression (or that you are depressed, or have been feeling depressed for some weeks and the feeling will not go away and it is impacting your life). This is may not be as easy as it sounds.

You might never have imagined yourself as able to be depressed or considered it possible to have depression. In your mind depression might have a stigma about it, as might any or all mental illnesses, which renders the occurrence of it in you as unthinkable, even abhorrent. Depressed people are mental health patients. Mental health patients spend their days sitting around smoking (probably cannabis) and otherwise wasting their lives. I am not one of those.

There are two things to say in response to this.

Firstly, the view of mental health patients sitting around

all day smoking is a stereotypical view. Like all stereotypical views it is inaccurate. True, some mental health patients do sit around and smoke all day. These tend to be the obvious ones. Many others wear suits, smart dresses, manage complex households and seem to us to live reasonably normal, even enviable, lives. Yet they are battling their own demons, hanging on as best they can and doing their best to look normal because our society demands normality and conformity. In other words, mental illness is more common than most people realize. Yet people do their best to hide it, to not to admit to it, to distance themselves from it.

That leads us to our second thing. Our own attitudes to mental illness are often (not surprisingly) heavily influenced by the attitudes to mental illness evident in our ambient society. After all, who is going to admit to something that other people despise and do their best to distance themselves from?

The question, of course, is rhetorical. So in admitting to our own mental illness we have to overcome the pervasive prejudice and discrimination of society against mental illness in general. In other words, we have got to swim against the flow, at a time in our lives when our ability to swim in any direction is being challenged by mental illness.

Think of it this way. As we live our lives we take on board a lot of stuff from people around us. Not all this stuff is good. Some of this stuff has to do with negative attitudes to mental illness. To admit we have depression we have first of all to overcome (echoes of Nietzscheism here) these negative external influences, and then counter them with an assertion of our own. This countering goes from inside you to the outside world, counter to the stuff coming at you and into you from the outside world. (Nietzsche calls this a will to power. I think it is a will, but I disagree with the power bit. But that is tangential to the discussion.)

How do we counter the negative influence of others? Again the strength to do this comes from within. There is an old saying (old sayings are old for a very good reason), the origins of which I do not know, which says that no-one can hurt you without your permission, or something to that effect. In other words the thoughts and influence of others in regard to depression, and especially our depression, can only hurt us if we allow them to. To avoid this, it becomes a matter of switching off from those influences, either by ignoring them (the harder thing to do) or by isolating yourself from them (the easier thing to do). This is why depressed people isolate themselves from others. Dealing with the negative attitudes of others at the same time as trying to cope with the fact of your depression simply becomes too hard. It is much easier to take yourself away to some dark little corner and reduce your existence to manageable levels, to stuff you can cope with, given that now you are not up to coping with much. This leads us to the next thing we can do.

Put bluntly, it is to seek help.

Let us be realistic here. Someone else is not going to get rid of your depression or solve all your problems or simply make you better. It is beyond them. Anyone who tells you they have all the answers simply does not even know what the questions are. But there are things people can do to help you.

Sadly, one has to be cautious when seeking help. The usual avenues we seek medical help from may not be that helpful. In some cases they can do more damage than good. I know of one general practitioner (family doctor) that said to his depressed patient, and I quote: 'You're in a dark place. Just turn the light on.' This is why when seeking help you need to adopt an attitude of 'if this person doesn't get it I will go to someone else until I find someone who does get it'.

This of course indicates that your general practitioner, or family doctor, is more than likely the first person you can turn to. It is, I think, more likely than not that your general practitioner will be helpful. But as I indicated caution is, sadly, necessary.

Presuming your general practitioner is helpful, what can he or she do to help you?

Let's look at this from the general practitioner's point of view. You turn up for a routine consultation (usually fifteen minutes) and complain that the bottom has fallen out of your world, you feel hopeless, there is nothing good in your life and you may even be thinking of ending your life because there is nothing good in it, there is only the endless repetition of negativity that is the hallmark of depression. Is your GP going to solve the problem in the ten remaining minutes? Of course not. So what can your GP do?

Firstly your GP has a responsibility to see that you are safe in the short term, that you are not going to go out and top yourself because there is no hope, and, or, that you are not going to succumb to anger and commit mass murder. The most immediate way to do this is for the GP to ask you to stay at the rooms until leaving them is a safe thing for you to do.

Secondly the GP may say, if they have their wits about them, that the bottom line is that no matter how hopeless you feel more people want you to stay alive than want you dead. This includes all members of the GP's practice (receptionists, nurses and other doctors). Even receptionists are trained to refer someone to a health professional immediately if they think there is a major risk of harm to that person.

I can personally vouch for this. When I had my first major breakdown I turned up unannounced at my doctor's rooms. The receptionist took one look at me (I didn't have to say anything) and got up from behind her desk and led me by the arm to a cubicle at the back, where a nurse was immediately informed of my presence. From that point on I was never left alone. I remember clearly thinking as she led me from the waiting room, 'Fuck, I must look bad!'

This makes the GP's offices a safe place for you.

Further, you may be surprised at the compassion people can show to those who feel everything is hopeless, providing they are aware how such people are feeling. People can only become aware if, of course, you tell them. Thus you need to articulate how you feel, even, or especially if, at the time, you do not feel like articulating anything to anybody.

Thirdly, the GP (or someone else from a mental health team) will usually prescribe medication. It is important to note that any medication for depression will help you (if it is suitable to you) cope with the depression, but it will not make the depression go away.

Fourthly, if things are really bad, a few days in respite care or admission to a mental health facility may be offered to you. If you are a clear danger to yourself and, or, to others this offer may be one you cannot refuse. Yes, that can happen. If this does happen remember that it is for everyone's good. Depression is not nice and dealing with it can involve major intervention. No-one said it was going to be as polite as a chat over a nice cup of tea.

The prescribing of suitable medication is almost a given. So what does suitable medication mean?

It will mean anti-depressants. How do they work?

I am not a pharmacological expert but I have swallowed a few (thousand) anti-depressants in my time.

There are five basic groupings of antidepressant drugs. With one exception, they all seem to work by enhancing neurotransmission in the brain.

The first, and by far the most common, type are known as SSRI's, meaning selective serotonin reuptake inhibitors. Serotonin is one of the main neural transmitters associated with depression. They carry messages across the synapses in the brain; in effect, SSRI's enhance neural communication; in our roads and traffic analogy they keep the traffic moving. Think green lights.

The name SSRI comes from how they work. They target serotonin, hence the "selective" part. But they work not by increasing the amount of serotonin, but by *increasing the amount of serotonin that effectively crosses the synapses.* How they do this is quite cool (I think, anyway).

I live in New Zealand. New Zealand has two major islands, the North Island and, unimaginatively, the South Island. The distance between the two islands is not great – think English Channel. There are ferry services running between the two islands. A ferry leaves the North Island for the South Island, crossing the strait between the two islands, which is known as Cook Strait. This sea route can be very rough at times, despite it not being very wide (I can personally attest to this!). Sometimes the sea is so rough the ferry cannot make the crossing and returns to its port of embarkation in the North Island. So far, this analogy is quite accurate, but this next part is simply for the purposes of the analogy and does not happen in real life. Because the ferries are specialist roll on–roll off ferries there are limited places they can dock. When the ferry gets back to the North Island, from whence it started its journey, it finds that all the berths are taken. Having nowhere to berth, the ferry *must* make the crossing across Cook Strait and so complete its journey.

The ferry is the serotonin. When the serotonin returns from attempting, but not completing, its journey across the synapses it also finds that its berth (the place it locks onto) is taken. (In medical terms the 'sending' neuron cannot take back up, or reuptake, the serotonin.) What is stopping the serotonin from being taken back up is a molecule from the anti-depressant drug that has the same locking mechanism (in the analogy, the roll on-roll off berth) as the serotonin. This molecule has filled up all the 'berths' at the sending axon terminal at which the serotonin might be taken back up and the serotonin, with no other place to go, heads back across the synapses to complete its journey. In this way neural transmission is enhanced.

This explains the 'reuptake inhibitors' part of SSRI. SSRI's have been something of the gold standard of anti-depressant medication for some time now. They are around under various names and brands (e.g., Prozac, which is branded as Fluoxetine) but they all work in generally the same way.

All medications have side effects, which can be thought of as doing things to your body other than the principal purpose of the medication. Because the human body is a classical chaotic system different medications have different side effects on different people. The occurrence of side effects is then difficult, if not impossible, to predict. Some occur with greater frequency than others and thus can be said to be more common, but it is impossible to accurately predict which medications will produce what side effects in which person. So when your GP says 'Try this and see how it goes', that is literally what he or she means. Trial and error is the only workable methodology here.

If the side effects are intolerable then you need to address this, and not put up with it for the cause of some nebulous greater good. While all SSRI's work in the same way, different brands have different formulations and it is simply a matter of trial and error to see which is right for you.

The positive effect of taking SSRI's is not apparent for some weeks (I've heard two weeks, I've heard six weeks, so go figure). Your GP (or prescribing doctor) should explain this to you.

The second type of anti-depressant is called a cyclic anti-depressant. These are usually classified as tricyclic or tetracyclic, depending on the number of rings (three or four) in their chemical structure. They also work by inhibiting the reuptake of serotonin and also norepinephrine (sometimes called noradrenaline), another neurotransmitter. (Norepinephrine can be thought of as a ferry from a different company in the analogy above.) Like the SSRI's, the aim is to improve communication between neurons, and so throughout your neural network. Nearly all anti-depressants work in this way. The difference between them can be one of efficacy but it is more likely to do with the occurrence of side effects. For example, a common tricyclic anti-depressant, amitriptyline, can sometimes affect bowel function.

Cyclic anti-depressants pre-date the SSRI's and are not so commonly used today. However a combination of cyclic anti-depressants and SSRI's can often have more beneficial outcomes for the patient than the use of one or other of these on their own. This has lead to a new type of anti-depressant which combines the two in one tablet. These medications are called Serotonin Norepinephrine Reuptake Inhibitors, or SNRIs. Effexor (known as Venlafaxine) is one of these.

Alternatively, a SSRI anti-depressant can be prescribed in combination with a cyclic anti-depressant, particularly if, as in my case, the side effects of an SNRI like Effexor are worse than the condition being treated. An advantage of this approach is being able to take the two respective types of medication at appropriate times. SSRIs are usually taken in the morning (mane in medical terms) and cyclic anti-depressants are usually taken at night (nocte in medical terms).

NASSA's, norepinephrine and specific sertoninergic antidepressants, work by enhancing the efficacy of the neurotransmitters epinephrine, norepinephrine and serotonin. They do this by blocking receptors in the same manner as SSRI's but they also prevent serotonin from working in unwanted areas (different sea routes in our analogy above) thus preventing many side effects that occur with SSRIs. This is where the *specific serotoninergic* bit of their name comes from.

The last group, MAOI's, work a little differently. There is an enzyme called monoamine oxidase which works to remove the neurotransmitters serotonin, norepinephrine and dopamine from the brain's chemistry. Less neurotransmission means more depression. Monoamine oxidase inhibitors basically stop this from happening. These (early) antidepressants are not much used these days because they come with the probability of significant side effects.

How long should you remain on anti-depressant medication? The most reliable answer that seems to be able to be given to this question is another question: How long is a piece of string? There is no methodical process or application that can determine how long you should remain on such medication. As a general guide it seems that the deeper rooted your depression is the longer you will need anti-depressant medication. If your depression is occasioned by a recent traumatic life event then it is possible that you will only need the medication until you recover from this trauma and get back on your feet. Accordingly the length of time on anti-depressant medication can be positively correlated with the severity of this trauma; in other words, the greater the severity the longer you may need the anti-depressant medication.

For deep-seated chronic depression you may be on anti-depressant medication for the rest of your life (as is the case with me). This means that instead of anti-depressant medication being viewed as a shorter term therapeutical input it is viewed rather as a supplementary input into the workings of your body and mind, just like food is an essential regular input to those same workings. It becomes to the depressed person as insulin is to the diabetic.

How does one differentiate between using anti-depressant

medication for a finite period of time and using it continuously, for the rest of your life? The basic answer is trial and error. A number of factors have input, including your medical history, the perceived depth of your depression, your response to the medication and your life context (for example, has your life changed so that the major stressor thought to be occasioning the depression has been removed, as in a change of job or career or spouse?). Some doctors work on some arbitrary rule that seems to make sense for them, such as if you present with symptoms of depression even after the second or third period of being on anti-depressant medication then long term or continuous use may be considered. But it is essentially a trial and error process. This is why it is most important to keep your doctor informed about what is happening. Doctors, like anyone else, are not mind readers. They know stuff about you because of what they observe (body language) but largely because of what you tell them. For example, if the anti-depressant medication you are on is giving you continuous headaches, yet you fail to communicate this to your doctor, then there is little the doctor can do about your headaches.

Your doctor should, of course, know all this and should, more importantly, inform you of most of this. Some (especially older) doctors are good on the knowing but not so good on the informing, their reasoning being that the patient doesn't really need to know what is going on. That attitude may have been acceptable when they were at medical school but it is not acceptable today. The primary medical ethic of autonomy, which says that you are in charge of your treatment, not your doctor, depends for good practice on you being informed about your treatment. You are, essentially, giving consent to putting complex chemicals in your body, so the consent you give (implicitly by accepting the prescription and following the instructions of your doctor) should always be *informed* consent. Not only *should* your doctor tell you what is going on, he or she *must* tell you what is going on.

It is not my intention that, after reading above about the pharmacological treatment of depression, you should know all there is know about that particular mode of treatment. To repeat myself, I am not a pharmacological expert on the treatment of depression, or indeed on the treatment of anything else. My intention here is that you have enough information in order that you may ask the right questions. What are the right questions? Simply, they are the ones you want answered.

What is it like, from the patient's point of view, being on

anti-depressants?

Anti-depressants take a while to kick in so any improvement in mood will happen gradually over time.

Further, for mild to moderate depression, anti-depressants may not be as effective as they were once thought to be. This simply illustrates that the whole field of psychiatric medicine is in a 'developmental stage' we might say, particularly if we are being polite.

While this in itself does not bother me (and of course, there is nothing I can do about it even if it did), what does bother me is mental health professionals making pronouncements about my condition and the treatment for my condition *as if those pronouncements were objective facts*. I have had the unsettling experience of being told one thing by one person and a few months or years later being told something completely different by another person. The reality is a lot of psychiatric medicine is little more than educated speculation, and a lot of the psychiatric drugs used in its practice (particularly, it seems, in relation to psychosis) were found to be effective (to some greater or lesser extent) simply by chance.

For the patient this means that, again, a certain caution is needed. At best it can be said that the drugs you are taking may help. It would be unwise to place total reliance on *just* the medication. Yet it remains that you are much more likely better off taking the medication than not taking it.

A major effect of anti-depressant medication, in my experience, is a levelling out of mood. You do not experience high or low moods to anywhere near the same extent as you probably did before taking the medication. This can make you feel a little numb. It can be frustrating when a beautiful sunset no longer excites in you feelings of awe, but it is also comforting when an unexpected setback no longer completely pulls the rug out from under you. Generally, life proceeds on a more even keel with the drugs than without them, and generally, this is a good thing.

This effect may be hard to notice as its onset is usually gradual. This can easily seduce the patient into thinking that he or she does not need the medication anymore and so stops taking it. All may go well for a while, even for some time, but the danger is that something like an unexpected setback will pull the rug out from under you. This is not a nice thing to happen. It puts you right back to square one, perhaps even further back than square one for the simple reason that every time the rug comes out from under you, it lowers the threshold at which the same thing can happen in the future. In short, with every adverse event you experience you become more vulnerable to adverse events.

So while you may not notice the effect of taking such medication, in all probability you will notice the effect of *not* taking the medication. Thus it is better to take it than not to take it.

Something else can happen when you take anti-depressant medication.

Imagine you have a headache. It is not a migraine or a severe headache, just a pervasive ache that you would be better without. You tell me you have a headache. I say to you, 'Here take this pill and then your headache will soon disappear.' So you take the pill and lo and behold, your headache disappears. As far as you are concerned it is a simple case of cause and effect. Ingesting the drug had the effect of making your headache go away. Later in the day we run into each other again (perhaps by the water cooler) and you say, 'Thanks for giving me that pill; it really cleared my headache up. What was it?' (Okay, there is a large degree of improbability to the story as no-one in their right mind is going to take a pill without knowing what it is, especially one handed to them by someone else, devoid of any identifying packaging. But just get over this improbability. It is a story. Good stories make a point or illustrate meaning or convey wisdom or some such stuff. They don't always have to be probable in order to do that. So back to the story.) 'What was it?' you ask. I reply, 'It was a sugar pill. It actually did nothing to cure your headache.'

'But my headache went away when I took the pill. Why was that?'

Why was that indeed. It is called the placebo effect. A placebo (in this context) is a substance, usually a sort of medication, given for a particular medical condition, which has no effect on that condition or any other condition, so that medically speaking, taking the medication is the same as not taking the medication. Placebos are widely used in clinical trials of drugs.

Let's say you want to test whether this new drug, which we might call D, is any good at treating the particular ailment A. So you get two groups of people together, all randomly selected, but with one thing in common. They all suffer from the ailment A and the severity of that ailment is documented before anyone is given any medication. To one group you give the new drug, D. To the other group you give a placebo that medically does nothing. Everyone is aware that one group gets the new drug D and the other group gets a placebo. But *no-one* is aware of which group gets what, so anyone in the trial does not know whether they have taken the new drug D or a placebo. After a course of treatment the severity of the ailment A is again documented for each person and the question is then asked, did the group that received the new drug D show a marked reduction in the severity of the ailment when compared to the group that was given the placebo? If the answer is Yes, the new drug works. If the answer is No then it is obviously pretty useless, at least in treating that particular ailment.

The reason one group (in technical terms, the control group) is given a placebo rather than simply not being given anything is counter the expectation in the other group that taking the drug will diminish the severity of the ailment. If everybody takes either the new drug or a placebo, and nobody knows whether they are taking the new drug or the placebo, then everybody has the same expectation of success. This eliminates the variable of expectation from the trial.

Put simply, the placebo effect says that if you think you will get better, you will.

Interestingly, the placebo effect seems to work even if you know you are taking a placebo. So in the story above, even if I had told you at the time when I gave the pill to you that it was a sugar pill and would have no pharmacological effect on your headache, your headache may still have gone away. Why? We don't know. But clearly the mind (the thinking part) has a role here, and clearly that role is not insignificant.

For those with a philosophy bent we are touching on the mind-body problem again.

The body (of which the brain is part) is made of particles (around 37 trillion I seem to recall from reading it somewhere) but the mind is *not* made of particles. The body and the mind are two different *types* of things.

We recall that the mind – body problem is concerned with *how* these two different *types* of things interact.

I suppose the whole mind-body thing could be summarized in the old saying of 'mind over matter'. This encapsulates the essence of the problem. But how does that help us in dealing with our depression?

The ability of the mind to exert some influence over our physical bodies is well documented, if not well understood. Hospital patients with a largely optimistic outlook generally recover more quickly than those with a largely pessimistic outlook. This is fine if the mind is healthy and the body is consequently encouraged to heal itself. (Much of medicine is simply about giving the body a chance to heal itself.) But what if the mind is *not* healthy?

We must realize that, to seemingly state the obvious, depression is a disease of the mind. The mind is not well understood, less so when it is afflicted with a disease like depression. (The reader may be drawn back to my comments about the efficacy of anti-depressant medication, and the conclusion implicit in those comments. Here I will state that conclusion explicitly in the hope of alleviating possible confusion. Depression is a disease of the mind. It can be treated (it is thought) by better facilitating communication between the neurons in the brain. But this is not to say that such a communication deficit (what some people have obliquely and quite ignorantly referred to as a chemical imbalance) is the *cause* of the depression. Were it was that simple. Pharmacology then only seeks to mitigate the effects of depression, not treat the cause of the depression.) So we are faced with the problem of a not well understood part of our human being that is in some sense diseased, that is, it is not performing to optimum efficiency, taking disease to mean literally 'not at ease'. The problem is compounded by the fact that our mind is central to our human being. In other words, the very 'thing' we are trying to use to make sense of our distress is the 'thing' that is distressed. In this sense mental illness is qualitatively different from other bodily illnesses. (There are, in my view, unfortunately still people, some even in the medical profession, who see depression either as just another illness to be treated like any other illness, or as not a real illness at all since its pathology cannot be linked to any physical causality. Stay clear of them. They simply have nothing to contribute to the treatment of depression and, or, the depressed person.)

The nature of the problem and the interplay between mind and body that we know goes on (even if we do not know *how* it goes on) gives rise to methodologies to mitigate the problem. Here I will introduce two new words: cognitive and behavioural. Anyone who has sought treatment for depression has probably been offered CBT counselling. CBT stands for Cognitive Behavioural Therapy. Cognitive refers to thinking, so that thinking influences behaviour. Behavioural (in the wider sense it is used here) refers to what you do (and what happens to you), which impacts on what you think.

An example. I feel good; therefore I will go for a walk on the beach. This is a cognitive operation. The 'feeling good' is a derivative of thought processes, which then leads to a particular behaviour (going for a walk on the beach). Note that the cognitive operation influences the behaviour. Now turn it around. I feel lousy, but if I go for a walk on the beach then I will feel better. Here the behaviour influences the cognitive process of feeling.

This is the essence of Cognitive Behavioural Therapy (CBT). Why? After all, cognitive behaviour therapy sounds learned, involved, up there so to speak – it even contains Latin (cogito). Let's look at it from a different perspective, from the perspective of the person actually suffering from depression.

From the point of view of the depressed person, there are two geneses of influence happening here. Each impacts, and therefore informs, the other but at the same time each has two distinct types of beginning.

One is a cognitive beginning. Our thoughts influence how we feel and how we behave. This process begins inside our minds and flows (so to speak) out to the external world, the world outside our minds, the world in which we behave, using the broadest meaning of that word. In the example above it is the first scenario, the 'I feel good' scenario which then leads to a particular behaviour (walking along the beach). We can visualize this process by thinking of a schematic person (I shall not insult your sensibilities by attempting to draw such a person) with an arrow coming out of her head, indicating that the genesis of thought and action lies within the person's mind and flows outward, thus influencing that person's behaviour and, consequently, that person's physical environment.

The other is behavioural, in the sense that it begins outside your mind, in your ambient environment. It simply flows the other way. In other words it flows from being external to the person (in the example above, the feel of the sand between my toes and the smell of salt in my nostrils) to being internal to that person, in other words to influence how that person is feeling (a cognitive operation).

Common sense suggests that every thought and action is a result of this dynamic interchange between internal and external.

This interchange continues all our lives. Neither our character, nor our thinking nor our behaviour is fixed at some point in our lives, to remain static thereafter.

I want to tease out the construct of this dynamic interchange. I want to look at what is internal to us (which I will define simply as what is inside our heads) and what is external to us (defined as the complement (in the technical sense of being everything other than) of what is inside our heads).

The observant reader will note that in defining what is external to us as being the complement of what is inside our heads I am in fact including our bodies (but not our minds) in this external categorization. This is intentional. That the demarcation between what is external and what is internal occurs at the mind – body interface (recall that we know the mind and the body interact; what we do not know is *how*) is simply a recitation of the age-old philosophical problem of the body and the mind.

So, we take internal to mean our thoughts and our thinking and external to mean everything that can influence our thoughts and our thinking, such as the physical sensations associated with going for a walk along the beach. We further posit one view of life as a dynamic interchange between the internal and the external that is set to continue throughout our lives. We take this to be a common sense view, since such an interchange is part of our adult experience of living. How does this help us cope with depression?

Our realization of how this can help us cope with depression will emerge out of a consideration of two further refinements of our internal – external interchange.

The first refinement recognizes that not only does this interchange take place throughout our lives, the dynamics of this interchange change throughout our lives, in ways that are generally predictable.

When we are young we learn largely through the ethic of consequence. If I do this, then this happens to me. For example, if I hit Susy with my toy tractor I will get my toy tractor taken off me. (Toy tractors are, according to my daughter the kindergarten teacher, weapons of choice, at least among the staff!) If I touch the fire I will get hurt. So we learn by consequence and we spend a number of years doing so. The consequences may change as we grow older (if I go really fast in my car the nice police person will come along and take it off me) but the learning methodology remains the same.

What is happening here is that what is external to us is dominating what is internal to us. Put simply, our experience of the world around us informs us about how we can cope with that world. In the dynamic interchange between external and internal the external is the dominant player. In philosophy this is called consequential ethics.

As we grow older we learn more about who we are as well as about the world around us. The balance between external and internal evens out, in broad terms. This is evidenced in our lives by our assumption of obligation.

In other words, now I do not only do things (or not do

things) because of the consequences of doing (or the not doing) those things, I now also feel a sense of obligation to do (or to refrain from doing) certain things. This sense of obligation may be instilled in us in any number of ways, but the key point is that it is instilled *in* us. Because of its internal genesis we exert more influence on the external world, and so the balance of the internal external dynamic evens up.

In philosophy this expression of a sense of obligation, of morality informed by reason and characterized by the phrase 'I should...', is known as the ethic of duty. The Categorical Imperative of the German philosopher Immanuel Kant is perhaps its finest expression.

As we grow older still, the balance shifts even further in favour of the internal over the external, such that the internal becomes dominant. This is expressed in such sentiments as who you are matters more than what you do; in the recognition of yourself by others as a person of character, as a person who says rather than 'I should...' as in the ethic of duty but 'I want to ...' or 'I must do this to be true to myself...' or similar words. Note that a person of character never describes themselves as a person of character. It is always a description assigned to that person by someone else. In other words, a person of character is of such character as to never assume he or she is indeed a person of character. Think of 'Honest John' the car salesman. If he is so bloody honest why does he need to tell you?

This emphasis on character finds its philosophical expression in Aristotelian ethics, in particular in Aristotle's *Nicomachean Ethics* (perhaps named after his son?) of circa 350 BCE. Aristotle developed a theory of Virtue (this part of ethics or moral philosophy is called 'Virtue Ethics') that emerges as the mean (in the sense of average) between two extremes. You can see what Aristotle meant by this by contemplating something as simple (and chaotic) as the weather. Some (few) days are very hot. Some (few) days (like today) are very cold. But most days are in between, one might say sort of average. Aristotle's doctrine of the mean is widely used not only in philosophy but in everyday life.

While this is not, as least as long as I can resist the temptation to make it so, a philosophical treatise I cannot help but pass an observation on philosophers. Here I have suggested a dynamic ethical template, moving from consequence to duty to character, moving from being externally dominant to internally dominant as we develop as human beings. But some, perhaps even most, moral philosophers insist that all ethics is grounded in only one of these templates, and of course they cannot agree on which one. Some (like Peter Singer, the Australian philosopher at Princeton) insist utilitarianism (following John Stuart Mill, the nineteenth century English philosopher), which demands the greatest good for the greatest number, is the only way to go. (Consequential ethics, mentioned above, arises out of utilitarian thought.) Some insist the ethic of duty is the way to go while a few advocate for virtue ethics.

I once encountered a philosophy tutor who insisted (to the point of rubbishing any alternative) that consequential ethics was the way, the truth and the life with all the fervour of a fundamentalist preacher. Indeed the only difference between him and a fundamentalist preacher was the content of his fundamentalism.

Anyway, back to depression. The second refinement has to do with the internal part of this internal – external dynamic interchange, what we call our mind, our cognitive activity. It illustrates the insidious nature of depression, a nature we have touched on before. Depression is an illness of the *mind*. When we use our cognitive, or internal, functioning to address our depression we are using the very 'thing' affected by our depression. How do we get around this?

We human beings have a trick up our sleeve, a trick it is thought that only human beings have. It is called in philosophy (in particular, the philosophy of the mind) second order thinking. It means we can think about what we are thinking about. Put simply it means we can discipline our thinking to step back from our immediate concerns and think about how we are responding to those concerns.

An example would be when you react to someone's assertion or statement with an 'off the top of your head' reply that at that particular moment seemed to you fairly sensible. But when you think later about what you said (and what you said is simply a representation of your primary thought) you realize it was inappropriate and you may, as a result of second order thinking, modify or even retract your initial response.

Another example occurs when a doctor or therapist asks you, 'Have you been thinking about suicide over the last week?' or some similar question. The question is about your cognitive activity, what is going on in your head, and to answer the question properly you are forced to reflect on what has been going on in your head over the last week; in other words to think about what you have been thinking about. (Leonardo DiCaprio may posit four levels of cognitive activity in the movie *'Inception'* but two are as good as it gets.) An example of second order thought is heard in the 1991 song by the American alternative rock group R.E.M., *'Losing My Religion'*, composed by Peter Buck. The chorus of the song contains the line *'I think I thought* I saw you try'.

How can all this help us with our depression?

Using this model of an external – internal dynamic interchange, one that tends to progress from external dominance to internal dominance as we develop as human beings, and putting this together with our capacity for second order thinking, we can come up with some strategies that will help us manage our depression. (From here on for simplicity I shall use only the first person, but every application of strategy to ourselves can be used by another person to help the depressed person.)

Our way into this is to reflect on the statement: What matters to us is what happens to us (external) *and* how we perceive what happens to us (internal). Remember the woman crossing the road? What she acted on was her perception, which sometimes coincided with reality and sometimes did not.

Let's start with what happens to us. Many of us think we

cannot control this, and this thought is especially common in depressed people. In terms of the big things, where we are born, who our parents are, our genetic inheritance, even our place in the world, there is some truth to this. We have to, as they say, play the hand we are dealt. But there are lots of little external things we can do to help manage our depressed mood.

Here are some suggestions. Please note that that is all they are. Some of them may be helpful for some people, others not so much. I certainly do not want to give the impression that if you do all these things your depression will magically go away. But I have found these strategies useful in managing my depression.

We can stick to a routine. This simple method of time management means we have fewer decisions to make and at the same time accomplish more than if we simply tried to make things up as we go. I have a particular morning routine which takes me through to having had breakfast, a shower and a shave and being dressed in clean clothes.

Attend diligently to matters of personal hygiene and grooming. There have been many mornings when I have not felt like having a shower at all but I make myself stick to my routine and have a shower, even, or especially, when I do not feel it is worth it.

We can choose to dress nicely. So often people are, or have been, told, in egalitarian New Zealand, that you need an excuse to dress up (usually a wedding or a funeral), otherwise to dress nicely is just being pretentious, a little up yourself. But dressing nicely (external) makes you feel better about yourself (internal). That in itself is sufficient reason to dress nicely.

Do things deliberately that make you feel better. For example, I feel lousy, but if I go for a walk along the beach I will better. Don't wait until you feel like going for a walk along the beach to actually go for a walk along the beach. And yes, exercise does help you manage depression. My daily walk is very therapeutic.

Do not put too many demands on yourself. This of course is easier said than done a lot of the time, particularly if children are involved. However, try to pace yourself and if you need a nap, take it. Dealing with depression is tiring.

It is also helpful if you do not allow other people to make demands on you for their own convenience. As I have learnt from experience this can lead to feelings of being taken for granted, being undervalued as a person, irritability and general grumpiness, none of which are particularly helpful in managing depression.

Terminate toxic relationships. This can be a hard choice to

make, particularly if the relationships occur in the context of close family. We are expected to get on with our sisters, brothers, mothers, fathers, sons, daughters and so on, but it is simply unrealistic for this to be the case every time. Sometimes these relationships become, or even have always been, somewhat toxic. A psychologist might be able to explain why this is so in a particular case (upbringing, environment, genetics, trauma...) but even then the relationship is still toxic. Hard choices have to be made, simply because the stakes here are high. It can become a choice between maintaining a toxic relationship because we think we should and having depression overwhelm us to the point of suicide, or terminating the relationship (thereby taking control of the situation) and managing our depression to the point where some quality of life is not only possible but even encouraged.

Do not expect people to understand what depression is like if they themselves have not experienced it. People just do not get it and no amount of explanation is going to make them get it. Putting this expectation on people is simply setting yourself up to fail. People's ignorance can often manifest to the depressed person as cruelty, a belittling both of the person and the illness. Some caution in who you talk to about your depression is called for. This extends even to health professionals. At best a competent mental health nurse might be expected to recognize that she or he does not understand what it is like to have depression. At worst, you and your illness are trivialized and you are left with a very strong impression that you must do what this professional has suggested and so help yourself. Often you are in no fit state to implement the behavioural changes suggested and then your depression is compounded by the guilt you feel at not being able to do something to help yourself. You can end up worse off than before.

There is a common theme running through all the suggestions I have made. It is all about taking control. As far as possible take control of your environment, the space you live in. Determine how you will groom yourself, how you will dress, the things you will do (and therefore, complementarily, the things you won't do), the people you see and talk to (and won't see and talk to) and so on. It is about making the space you live in better, safer and more supportive for *you.*

Make a plan of what to do if you feel that everything is turning to custard. This is a plan of last resort if you will. It should necessarily involve seeking help. This is okay. We all need help from time to time, and not just with our mental health. This can include phoning a trusted friend, or presenting yourself at the local Emergency Department and saying you are suicidal, or presenting to the local public mental health centre during business hours, or calling an ambulance or ringing a mental health crisis number. Part of your plan can include entering the local mental health crisis number into your phone and/or cell phone (it is usually a toll free call) just in case of the eventuality of everything going to custard.

The best thing to do is either present yourself at the local public mental health centre (during business hours) or, because crises are no respecter of business hours, ring the mental health crisis number or present yourself at the local Emergency Department. It is important to convey to whomever you speak to that this is a mental health emergency. This may not be obvious to the person assessing you, sadly the more so the younger that person is.

Usually the first person you see will expect you to tell them what is wrong but the nature of your emergency (suicidal depression) makes it difficult to communicate. One way around this is to carry a small card or note (easily made on a home computer) that has your name, address and phone number on it and the words *'This is a mental health emergency'* written on it. Simply hand over the card.

A word or two about presenting to the local public mental health centre.

Firstly, in New Zealand, you need to make sure it is the centre run by the local health board. Private mental health service providers can be very good but they usually do not do crisis intervention work. I am sure such a distinction between crisis intervention work and ongoing support of mental health patients is made in other western societies also.

Secondly, the mental health centre should see you the same day. They usually have emergency appointments during the day for just such eventualities as you are experiencing.

Thirdly, if you are seen by a health board mental health service there will undoubtedly be flow on consequences. One can be admission. If this is what needs to happen then so be it. Forget about stigma and what other people think or might think and what your family thinks or might think. The stakes are high. Suicide is not something you can undo. It is a one way street.

Another and perhaps more likely consequence is that the mental health service will say 'This is what we are going to do' and outline to you a plan of action. This will almost always involve them in contacting you the next day. *You have a right to expect that the service does what the service says they will do.* If they do not do what they say they will do (yes, it does happen) then take proactive action. In other words if they haven't contacted you then you contact them. If after taking proactive action they still haven't got back to you (yes, that happens too and I am speaking from experience) then you need to communicate this to someone a bit further up the food chain. In my case, I emailed the health board Chief Executive Officer. Within fifteen minutes the mental health service was on the phone apologizing all over the place. Two hours later the CEO himself rang me (earning my respect for him and for the system in general) to check that his mental health service had done what they had obviously told him they were going to do. As I said before, the stakes are high. This is not tiddlywinks.

A similar attitude is preferable if you present to the local Emergency Department. Sadly, if you expect the welcoming arms of compassion and understanding to be extended by the health professionals on duty then in all likelihood you will be disappointed. Part of this is, I think, because what you see as an emergency they may see as less urgent, perhaps not even an emergency at all. At triage (your first assessment on arriving at an Emergency Department) you may be redirected to an after-hour's doctor on the basis that your case is not an emergency and this is the Emergency Department. Stay put. Repeat calmly that this is a mental health emergency (or present the little card saying the same thing) and that you have a right to be seen by professional staff. Do not be fobbed off by someone who has no idea what you are going through.

Once you get through triage you will eventually be seen by a junior doctor. If it is the middle of the night you will get whatever 'teenage' doctor was unlucky enough to pull night shift. In my several visits to the local Emergency Department the tone of the duty doctor was at most times condescending, implicitly wondering why I was wasting his or her time. (This has since changed, presumably because the CEO of the health board put my above mentioned e-mail on my file for all to see. The change in attitude apparent on my last visit to the local Emergency Department sadly confirms that those who know how the system works and know what to do when things do not go well are at an advantage over people who wouldn't dare challenge the authority of a health professional or a health system. It should not be like this, but human nature being what it is, it is like this.)

If you have a relatively minor physical ailment, but are struggling to cope with it, it is more likely than not that a junior doctor will focus on your minor physical ailment rather than on your inability to cope. It must be made clear that it is your inability to cope that constitutes the emergency, for the simple reason that if you are depressed and for whatever reason you reach the limit of your ability to cope, then you are desperate to end your distress. And there are only two ways to do that.

One is to end the distress by ending your own life.

The other is to seek help.

While any reasonable person would say that the latter course of action is preferable, taking that course of action can in itself add to your distress if you are not pertinacious in seeking help.

While we have mentioned before (Chapter 4) that you are responsible for dealing with your own depression, doing this effectively can involve a level of determination that can often seem beyond the depressed person, especially, as we have just considered, when exercising that responsibility involves enlisting the help of others. Like the spiralling downward of cause and effect which then interchange so that one becomes the other, the need to seek help is undermined by the hindrance to seeking help occasioned by the effects of the depression itself, which then heightens the need to seek help.

Specifically I am talking about withdrawing from some or even most aspects of everyday life in order to take control of your space, which includes responsibly seeking the help you need. In military terms I suppose it would be called a retreat and regroup. There is both an encouragement and a caution here.

The encouragement is cased in the reduction of external influence to a manageable level. Put simply, there is too much stuff coming at you and you feel the need to withdraw to a place where all this stuff simply cannot get to you. That is fine in itself, for it is simply a survival mechanism. Such a withdrawal will (I hope) encourage your survival.

The caution here has to do with the withdrawal. Isolating yourself may limit the amount of external stuff you have to deal with but it also limits your reception of the good external stuff that can help you. This is the reason part of your survival strategy of withdrawal should always include some form of help-seeking. The rub is that at the very time you do not feel like seeking help, or even talking to anyone, that is the time when it is imperative to do so. It is easy to entertain suicidal thoughts which are born of frustration and a sense of there not being a way out. Continued isolation fuels this frustration and these thoughts. By seeking help, in the ways mentioned above, you stop being isolated and consequently the negative thinking fuel led by isolation becomes dis-empowered.

Let's move now to our perception of what happens to us. This is the cognitive part of cognitive behaviour therapy and has to do with what goes on inside our heads.

We will employ two approaches to cognitive therapy. The first has to do with the difference between what we perceive and what actually is, if anything can be said to be 'actually is'.

The second has to do with first order and second order thinking. Remember that second order thinking is essentially thinking about what we are thinking about, and we assume that only human beings have this capability.

Let's take a moment to consider just what is inside our heads. Our brain is the most complex thing we know of in the entire universe. It is that simple. It is a product of around four million years of evolution and like every living thing is still evolving.

But depression is a disease of the *mind*. This observation

emphasizes the difference between our brain and our mind. The online dictionary, Dictionary.com, suggests the brain serves to control and co-ordinate our mental and physical actions. The mind, on the other hand, is perceived by the same dictionary to be the element, part, substance, or process that reasons, thinks, feels, wills, perceives, judges, etc. Latterly the mind has come to be thought of as our consciousness, the 'picture' of ourselves and the outside world our brain paints for us. To use the language of the definitions provided, we might think of the brain as controlling our (for our purposes) mental actions while the mind *is* those mental actions.

As I have already said the relationship between the brain and the mind, or our consciousness if you prefer the latter term, is not well understood. If a thought is produced by a particular arrangement of particle matter in the brain, does that thought replicate itself if in, for example, one of Brain Greene's parallel universes where an exact copy of that same brain is functioning and therefore replicating that exact arrangement of particle matter?

So what do we know about the mind and the brain? Let's take a look at what goes on in our heads, using the analogy of a digital camera hooked up to a computer so that the computer's screen displays what the camera 'sees'.

The camera sees an object, let us say a chair. The camera translates the reception of photons facilitated by its lens into electrical signals which it then sends along the wire connected to the computer. The processing part of the computer (its innards, we might say) receives those signals and reconverts them back into photons to be emitted from the computer's screen. Thus the chair appears on the computer screen.

In this little analogy the camera is your eye, the wire to the computer is your optic nerve, the computer innards are the occipital lobe of your brain (located at the back of your head) and the computer screen represents the picture your brain has created for your mind to see.

Exactly the same process goes on for the other four senses of sound, smell, touch and taste, but for simplicity's sake we will stick with the consideration of sight.

If this process of transmission of information from your eye to your brain in order to create something that your consciousness is aware of is what we might call linear, that is, if an image of a chair translated into electrical signals (into the binary code of electrical transmission) is recreated exactly as it was received then we would always produce in our consciousness an exact replica of what the eye is 'seeing'. (If you are philosophically minded, you might note that this process of transmission takes time; it takes time for the eye to convert the information into an electrical signal, for that signal to travel to the brain and for the brain to replicate that information in your consciousness. Not much time, but it does take *some* time. The point is, you always 'see' things as they *were*, not as they *are*. In other words, you are always behind the times. Dammit, your kids were right!) However our brain does not replicate the signal exactly.

Firstly there are limits as to the amount of information that can be transmitted in this way. If you watch a movie on the big screen you will perceive the motion as continuous. In fact the 'continuous' motion is a series of still pictures, in sequence, shown at the rate of twenty-four frames per second. (For those with an interest in theoretical physics this is a nod to Heisenberg's uncertainty theorem. This theorem emerged long before he was a meth cook in Albuquerque!) At this rate, your brain *perceives* continuous motion even when your eye does not see it.

Secondly, because it takes time for this process to occur, the brain takes shortcuts. It receives part of the information from the eye and then (metaphorically speaking) fills in the gaps from its memory, say from a previous time of 'seeing' the chair. (This is why older people, who have bigger memories, can read situations much faster than younger people.) This is all well and good, except for one consideration: what if the brain gets it wrong?

To use our previous example of a woman crossing the road, when she looks down the road the brain fills in a picture of what she expects to see. If her glance down the road is impetuous the brain may well rush to fill in the gaps according to what she expects to see – an empty road. The electrical signals emanating from the photons from the approaching car are ignored and the picture created in her consciousness is that of an empty road. Accordingly, she steps out on the road, only to be hit by the car she literally did not see. (This is also why eye witness accounts of events can be somewhat unreliable.)

The brain's input here can include, as well as things that are there but it does not 'see', things that are *not* there but it *does* see. This is the origin of hallucinations, not only of sight but also of auditory (for example, hearing voices), tactile (for example, things crawling on my skin when there are no things crawling on my skin), olfactory and gustatory sensations. In psychological jargon, this is referred to as psychosis.

What has this got to do with depression? Two things. Firstly, what we think (perceive, speculate) is or might be happening *is not necessarily the case.*

Secondly, we can consider what really is going on (as far as our cognitive abilities allow us) by using our ability for *second order thought.*

These two considerations are exemplified in our story about the woman crossing the road.

In the second version of that story the woman looks to see that the way is clear and perceiving that it is she proceeds to cross the road. However her brain got it wrong and she is hit and killed. What she thought was happening (the road being clear of traffic) was simply not the case. So those negative thoughts you think everyone has about you (or even that you have about yourself) simply need not be the case.

In the third version of that story the woman's brain again incorrectly perceives the way is clear and she proceeds to cross the road in the face of oncoming traffic. But this time her friends intervene and stop her in her tracks because they have rightly seen that the way is *not* clear. External intervention can help us reconcile what we perceive with what actually is, usually and especially just when we need it. In the absence of her friends what might have happened?

She may have simply repeated the second scenario (being hit by the oncoming car) or she may have decided to pause and check her initial perception that the road was clear using her second order thought ability. In other words, she may have gone through a thought process that went something like, 'I see the road is clear, but let me pause and double check just to make sure'.

We can look at this another way. We can differentiate between what happens to us and what we *think* of what happens to us. For example a minor car crash might be just a nuisance to one person, while to another it may be a traumatic event which affects their confidence when driving. The same *external* event can have widely varying *internal* consequences for different people. Similarly a bad day at work for one person may well become a question about one's suitability for that particular occupation for another. And so a negative external event (for example, your spouse leaves you) may be internalized quite differently by different people. Realising *how* you internalize it involves your capacity for second order thought.

Exploring your second order thought can be done by 'talking' your thinking, literally reflecting on that thinking out loud. This is best done in the context of a conversation with a trusted person. The trusted person needs to be a good listener. That is, they need to suppress their own thoughts and feelings and simply reflect back to you what they understand to be your thoughts and feelings. By checking what is reflected back to you with what you are thinking or feeling and seeing to what extent there is agreement between the two you can then see for yourself whether you are making any sense or not (if you do not your listener will not comprehend what you are saying), what sense you are making of what you think or feel (what is accurately reflected back) and therefore be in a position to disparately analyse what you are thinking or feeling (when you think about what is reflected back to you by your trusted listener).

This of course is the realm of the counsellor, and specifically the realm of cognitive therapy. We need to be very clear that the primary job of a counsellor is to listen empathetically. This involves a putting aside of the counsellor's imperative to give advice or worse, to meet his or her own needs. Sadly, many counsellors are in counselling simply to meet their own needs, which are often some form of needing to be needed, of wanting people to be dependent on them. I repeat, the primary function of having counselling is to be listened to empathetically. If this does not happen, then whatever else may happen is unlikely to be of any help and may actually be of some harm.

In terms of our external – internal dynamic, cognitive therapy has to do with the internal part of that dynamic. It may be thought of as taking your thoughts and feelings out and having a good look at them, and then putting them back with any necessary therapeutic adjustments made.

There is a sense in which this external – internal dynamic can be considered as 'overcoming'. What I mean is that the long term (years) object of this dynamic is for the internal part of the dynamic to overcome the external. What this means is that you are not any longer defined by things external to you, rather your view of your self is better determined by your own consciousness overcoming the external influences coming at you throughout most of your (especially younger) life. This means that your consciousness (self, mind, being) influences you and, consequently, your ambient environment, rather than you being primarily influenced by it.

In popular culture we recognize this by saying that he or she is his or her *own* person (in other words, a person who does not simply react to other people or circumstances, but one who influences those people and circumstances). The negative correlation of this is saying that this person is, for example, 'always at the beck and call of others'. In philosophy this idea of overcoming is the cornerstone of Nietzschean philosophy of the late nineteenth century. Friedrich Nietzsche advanced the idea of the 'ubermensch' which is sometimes translated from the German as 'superman' but is better translated (according to the Princeton Nietzschean scholar Walter Kaufmann) as 'overman', that is, as one who overcomes. (Nietzsche no doubt intended his ubermensch to refer to anyone, man or woman, who overcame, but gender neutral language was not important in nineteenth century Europe.) The application of the Nietzschean philosophical idea of overcoming to the context of cognitive therapy for depression is probably not specifically intended by Nietzsche but does seem to me a valid application, especially given the psychological basis of Nietzsche's philosophy. Nietzsche himself suffered from depression, though it is now reasonably thought that this may have been a side effect of an undiagnosed and therefore untreated brain tumour behind his right eye. (The diagnosis recorded in his medical records is syphilis, contracted by contagion, but nineteenth century medicine was hardly an exact science, if a science at all. Almost anything could be diagnosed as syphilis if the doctor could not determine any alternate diagnosis.)

The idea of 'overcoming' when applied to the treatment and management of depression seems to me to powerfully underline the core therapeutic intent in dealing with depression. It means that depression does not control you, the depression sufferer, but rather you exert control over the depression by exercising strategies (both behavioural and cognitive) to deal with that depression.

The preference for the internal over the external indicates a process, a struggle which may take years. It is thus important when considering how to treat and manage your depression to take a long view. There are no swift cures, no magic pills or potions to quickly deal with depression. To deal with depression is to be in there for the long haul.

Depression may be episodic or pervasive. It seems to be either one or the other. In other words you may have bouts of depression interspersed with periods that are relatively depression free. Or you may have a chronic depression that pervades every aspect of your being for the rest of your life. Either way, the strategies for dealing with depression remain much the same. What differs are the frequency and the way you implement those strategies to treat and manage your depression.

The core strategy in dealing with your depression can, I think, be summed up in the phrase 'taking control'. This does not mean denying your depression and pretending it is not there, nor does it mean attacking your depression and beating it down with some form of blunt instrument. It means living with your depression (or, if your depression is episodic, the possibility of a depressive episode occurring) and managing it in such a way that you have the depression, rather than that the depression has you. While this is true for all illness (and indeed, for all adversity) the thing with depression is that your mind (consciousness, being, sense of self, etc.), which you are using to make this distinction between depression having you and you having depression, is the very thing affected by depression. I hope I have conveyed ways to deal with this.

We must be realistic and say that not everyone who suffers from depression is going to have the ability to mount a strategy of overcoming, in terms of the internal overcoming the external dynamic I have posited above.

Some people will always be, to a greater or lesser extent, at the mercy of their depression and there is little other people can do about this. In other words, in some people's lives it is simply unrealistic to expect the internal to overcome the external in any way. For them, the external will always dominate. This is okay. It is, again, just another situation that has to be dealt with. But how?

In the internal external dynamic I have posited above I speak of the internal overcoming the external. This suggests the two are in conflict.

In dealing with depression I have argued the desirability of withdrawing to a safe place, a place with manageable external stimuli and influence, as a way to gather one's internal self together, as it were.

Let's put these two things together.

Let's posit a scenario where a depressed person is helped to withdraw to safe place, a place where the external stimuli are largely managed by empathetic able people. The external stimuli now become 'friendly' to the depressed person rather than hostile as the depressed person usually encounters them. The external stimuli are still dominant but now someone has stepped in and artificially filtered out the hostile stimuli, actively replacing them with 'friendly' stimuli. (In our story of the woman crossing the road this is indicated by the other women in the group stepping in to prevent the woman from stepping out in front of the car.)

This can be done, for example, by providing sheltered accommodation for the person, by providing assistance with the myriad demands of day to day living, providing regular contact with mental health professionals and therefore generally providing them with assistance to live in the community.

There are many private charities that do this sort of thing in New Zealand and seem to do it very well. (The alternative of course is the dreaded institutionalization. I don't think any of us want to go back there.) Such assisted living is for some people as good as it is going to get. And that is okay. That our society provides such assisted living to vulnerable people is itself indicative of a societal, rather than a personal, strategy of overcoming.

I want to finish this chapter by making a specific comment about existential depression. This depression has its genesis in the perception that one's existence is essentially futile, we might say beyond redemption, *and* that there is nothing that can be done to change that. This sort of depression was prevalent in Germany in the years following the Second World War when the German people were forced to come to terms with the horrors their nation had inflicted upon the world.

In answer to a question asked in this context of post war

Germany, 'What (will) posterity think when it thinks about us?' the character Peter Gutman in Christa Wolf's autobiographical novel *'City of Angels'* replies, 'Maybe people will say: In the end they lived without illusions but not without remembering their dreams. Remembering the wind of utopia in the sails of their youth.'[10] Is this a description, even a definition, of the self-redemption the depressed person seeks? To remember the dreams of youth despite having one's illusions about the world shattered? Can this be the basis of hope for the depressed person?

This brings us to the question of how do you help someone with depression.

---

[10] Christa Wolf, *'City of Angels'*, p. 240 in the first American edition (pub. 2013).

## 6.     How do you help someone with depression?

This question is naturally concerned with relationships. It is in my mind asked by people who have some sort of interpersonal relationship with someone who has depression. It may be a familial, romantic, casual, sexual or friendly relationship, or some combination thereof, but it is some sort of relationship. Further, rather than a strategy of relation to all people who suffer from depression, my intent here is to explore the ability of another person to help someone with depression in the context of a one-to-one relationship. It is also my intention that this context should *not* include the (hopefully therapeutic) relationship between a counsellor and his or her depressive client. I have touched on the special nature of this relationship in the previous chapter.

There is an obvious necessity to consider how one person may help someone with depression in somewhat general terms, as I simply cannot anticipate the nuances of each and every such interpersonal relationship. This suggests a need to take these considerations not with a grain of salt but rather with an appreciation that they cannot be definitive of every such interpersonal circumstance. Some considerations will thus be more relevant to the reader than others. Which ones are more relevant and which ones are less so will depend on the particular circumstance that the reader is involved with or has knowledge of. Thus the question of relevancy must necessarily be one for the reader to consider.

My approach to this question is philosophical. It has to do with the nature of human *being*. This is not simply because I am of a philosophical turn of mind although I suspect that has more to do with it than I either realize or admit to. It is because depression annihilates ones being. It sucks the flavor out of life. It reduces Life (with a capital L) to a mere existence. It takes away meaning and replaces it with emptiness. And it does so day after day after day, until mere existence is the only existence the depressed person knows. The motivation for continuing that existence has completely gone. Suicide can be seen as the only way out, the only way to end this existential agony.

Consequently my approach here is to address ways in which the spark of Life, some sort of meaning beyond mere existence, can be rekindled in the context of an interpersonal relationship.

It necessarily implies that the other person in such a relationship, the person who may ask the question which titles this chapter, is not only not themselves depressed, but has some insight into the nature of their particular human being. This may sound grand and 'deep' but it simply means that this person has a handle on what matters, both generally in regard to human being and in particular with regard to their own being. In other words this person (you?) has thought about, and in some way can articulate, the value and sanctity of human life by having regard for the value and sanctity of *their* life. (If this sounds familiar that is because it probably is. In the holy writings we know as the Gospels Jesus of Nazareth suggests that as we love ourselves, so we need to love our neighbour. This is not an incursion of religious doctrine into the text. Jesus was simply reiterating a philosophical truth that was already extant in his world, one which came to be known as the 'Golden Rule' (unless you are a Presbyterian, in which case the Golden Rule is 'He who has the gold makes the rules.').)

It then follows that when you have regard for the sanctity and value of your life, you can encourage others to have regard for the value and sanctity of *their* lives. As we noted in Chapter 4, you cannot do this for them. It is something they must do for themselves. We can encourage, yes, but we cannot live the life (Life?) of another person for them. Each of us is an autonomous entity.

It further follows that helping someone with depression must conform to the internal – external dynamic we have explored in the previous chapter. Just because we are now concerned with helping the depressed person, rather than the depressed person invoking strategies to help themselves, does not negate this dynamic. It simply alters the perspective from which we look at it. Specifically, we will be looking to mitigate the external influences on the depressed person at the same time as encouraging the internal dynamic to express itself, to gain some traction as it were.

This division of the depressed person's interaction with the world will form the basis of our approach here. We will look at ways to mitigate the external influences on the depressed person so as not to inflame or feed the depression the person suffers, influences that may impact negatively on the being of the depressed person, and we will look at ways of encouraging the depressed person to recover, recognize and express his or her own sense of being.

First of all, a few don'ts. I do not like don'ts (yes I know that is a recursive sentence) but sometimes it is important to begin a consideration of what we can do with a nod to the relevancy of the things we should not do, and I think this is one of those times.

Let's be blunt.

Do not tell the depressed person to 'harden up' and just get over it. You may as well give them a loaded gun and tell them to get on with it.

Do not say to the depressed person that it is 'all in your head'. The depressed person already knows this. Of course it is all in his or her head. That is the problem. The depressed person would very much like to get it *out* of his or her head. All you're doing is belittling the depressed person by telling them something they themselves are painfully aware of.

Do not issue ultimatums that essentially have a 'no win' result, for example, 'Sort your shit out or I am leaving you.' What will invariably happen is that the depressed person tries, but fails, to 'sort his or her shit out' because such sorting just cannot be done at such short notice over such a short time period implied in the ultimatum. There are only two possible outcomes. Either you did mean what you said and you leave (probably depriving the depressed person of the last remnant of support), or you didn't mean what you said and you stay, meaning that the depressed person now no longer knows if he or she can trust anything you say.

Do not tell a depressed person that 'no-one else has this crap to put up with'. Apart from anything else, you will almost certainly be wrong. A lot of people either struggle with depression themselves or live in some sort of relationship with someone who struggles with depression. You are simply not aware of this.

The effect on the depressed person of being told that no-one else has this crap to put up with is massive guilt followed by considering themselves beyond the societal norms of everyday life. Therefore they are 'different'. This is illustrated by the common experience of depressed people (and those who are trying to help them) walking through, for example, a shopping mall and thinking to themselves 'no-one else feels like I do, no-one else has to put up with this unending negativity' when in fact it is almost certainly not the case.

You probably by now get the picture. There are no quick fixes, no sledgehammers nor any instant wonderful psychological cures that deal to depression the way you can deal to, for example, a broken door.

Consideration of what not to do also suggests we have some awareness of the toll living with and, or, dealing with a depressed person takes on another person. The 'don'ts' I have exemplified above are often indicators of frustration and of a general feeling of being entirely fed up with the depressed person and their depression, particularly if, for example, they do not get out of bed or wash or otherwise do something – anything!- to help themselves.

So what do you do when you reach the end of your tether and you seriously want to scream stuff at the depressed person and even throw stuff at them?

Those of us who are parents and who have had (or have) 'hands on' experience of parenting babies and small children will recognize how quickly (often diligent) parents can reach the end of their tether with a baby that just will not stop crying or a child on to their third tantrum in the space of half an hour. The advice rendered in these cases is the same advice I would counsel for the frustrated 'partner' (in the widest possible sense of that term) of a depressed person.

Walk away.

Remove yourself from the source of your frustration. Take yourself off to some place that you find quiet, comforting, consoling – in short, some place that enhances your human being rather than detracts from it.

This may sound cruel and hard-hearted. It may even be cruel and hard-hearted. Unfortunately these considerations must not, in my opinion, sway our resolve to remove ourselves from the source of our frustration before some sort of meltdown of our own begins to occur. Simple logic dictates that one person having a meltdown is better than two.

There is one crucial difference between the parent – child relationship stretched to breaking point and the interpersonal relationship between a depressed person and someone wanting to help them similarly stretched. In the parent child – relationship the parent(s) have a familial (and, in New Zealand and in Western society generally, legal) responsibility for the child's care and welfare. For example when a parent walks away from a screaming baby he or she must ensure the baby is in a safe environment and be available to intervene if there is any indication the baby becomes unduly distressed; such distress may indicate a medical problem. The same is true if there is any threat to the baby's environment. This is because the baby is dependent on the parent.

Such dependence is not, or perhaps more correctly should not, be a hallmark of the interpersonal relationship between two adults. No matter how close an interpersonal relationship may be there can be no suggestion that one person is, or should be, dependent on the other. This is particularly so when one person in the relationship is vulnerable as a result of, in our context, depression.

To accept this is a big ask. It seems to go against everything that we have been encouraged by society to do, that is, to care for those close to us. But the key thing in this consideration, in my opinion, is the realization that the depressed person is also an autonomous adult human being. To try to take that autonomy away from them, or even to expect that you, the helper, will succeed in imposing a rational discourse on the depressed person, is simply doomed to failure.

This realization presents itself in society in phrases like 'It was his choice' or 'I cannot think for her'. Too often theses phrases are heard in the aftermath of a suicide. The act of suicide may have been a stupid course of action but the hard reality of suicide is that an autonomous human being made a specific choice to end his or her own life. We can ruminate for hours, days and weeks on end about why this person made that choice, but the fact of him or her making that choice is now historic.

Does this mean we must 'condone' the act of suicide as an active choice of an autonomous human being? No. The intentional and unnecessary killing of any human being is in my opinion abhorrent. Whether this killing is done by the human being's own hand or the hand of someone else is irrelevant. The sanctity of life is paramount.

But the point I am ever so gently trying to make is that if we take away the autonomy of a human being (in which they make decisions for themselves) we have in effect taken away a significant part of their being. In some respects we have killed them anyway.

The point is made in full cognizance of the view that suicide is *completely* preventable, as articulated by some researchers working in the area of suicide prevention. Further, the point would seem to contradict the view that *all* suicides are preventable. How might we reconcile these varying viewpoints?

I take issue with the view that *all* suicides are preventable. Most, yes. The great majority, sure. But not *all*. Words like *completely* and *all* are absolute words. They allow no dissent, no exceptions. It is my view that words such as these are dangerous in the nebulous field of mental health. I further acknowledge that autonomy is one of the four primary medical ethics, going further to acknowledge that autonomy is both a subject and an object of medical ethics. In other words, medical practice should have as its aim the preservation and enhancement of autonomy. In my view this means that  the person is treated, not simply the illness or injury.

The conclusion here, then, is that while we may (almost certainly) disagree with the act of a person in taking their own life and while with the right intervention at the right time the act of taking one's own life may well be able to be prevented, we cannot in good conscience take the choice of suicide away from someone, simply because we cannot be, or become, responsible for another autonomous human being. We can encourage them not to make that choice and we may do so by presenting alternative courses of action but we cannot *think* for them.

(It remains, however, that if a person is deemed a danger to themselves or to others they can be placed in appropriate care, against their will, for their own protection and the protection of others. This could be construed as taking the choice away from them. In this circumstance we argue that the person is not acting responsibly and therefore has ceded their autonomy to a responsible person. This is exactly the situation for dementia patients who quickly become unable to make choices in their own best interests.)

There is a consequence to our conclusion and it is this consequence I am aiming for. To restate the above in a different way, it is the harsh reality of suicide from depression that a person has made (in their view) a rational choice to end their own life. That is their choice and it simply reflects the autonomy of their being. We who are close to that person cannot be held, by ourselves or by others, responsible for that choice.

I have emphasized this point because I have talked with many survivors of suicide (by survivors of suicide I mean those left behind after someone has taken their own life) and the number one thing all these survivors have in common is guilt, occasioned by their perception that they could have done something to prevent the suicide. Comments like 'If only I knew what he was going through' or 'If I was a better husband (wife / partner / son / daughter / mother / father etc.) then this would not have happened' abound.

This is why I think the mantra that suicide is *entirely* preventable needs to be taken with a grain of salt. If you accept this mantra and then a person close to you commits suicide following depression, the guilt you will then undoubtedly feel at not being able to prevent that suicide will be devastating.

But for all that there are things that can be done to mitigate the risk of suicide from depression. (Not all suicides result from depression, but suicide can too easily be seen as the default option when one is the grip of depression.) We shall come to those in a moment.

It is easy, in the aftermath of a suicide (and I know from experience, there is a huge aftermath), to accede to feelings of guilt and fall prey to a flood of 'if only' questions. They are not helpful. There is no sense in which they can be helpful. The tragedy of suicide is that it tends to generate questions which can only be answered by the person who has just died. This is a no win situation. All that consideration of these questions accomplishes is to beat up on the person asking them, at a time when that person is no doubt feeling lousy enough already.

It is not easy to dismiss these feelings. To do so we must see them in the wider context of the death of an autonomous human being by his or her own hand. To do this takes time, energy and effort, often in huge quantities.

I cannot stop any person from having these feelings following the suicide of a person close to them.

But I can say, it doesn't end with these feelings. That is the point I have so carefully tried to make.

So, what about some stuff that you can do to help the depressed person? To put it another way, what are some of the things we can do to mitigate the risk of suicide from depression for someone close to us?

I will list a number of things that may be helpful,

depending on context, but my list will invariably head toward one conclusion about what is ultimately helpful. I can anticipate your question. Wait and see.

Be gentle with the depressed person. Low voices, quiet spaces, kids told to play outside, visitors put off, loud intrusive people avoided – you get the picture. Stillness and calm are what helps the depressed person. There is enough turmoil in their head without adding to it by way of external stimuli.

Allow the depressed person some space and some latitude. Being closed in has the same effect as being in a noisy turbulent environment. If the depressed person wants to sit on a rock in the garden, or a bench in the park, or on the back porch or wherever, so be it. The depressed person is looking for a place that they find quiet and comfortable, a place that is not threatening, a place where they feel isolated from, and thus safe from, the everyday hustle and bustle of life, a place where they have some control over what happens and perhaps more importantly, over what doesn't happen. Allow the depressed person to withdraw to this place and perhaps even encourage this by surreptitiously providing the space and the opportunity for such a withdrawal.

Accept that the desire of the depressed person to withdraw to a safe place is *not* the same as not wanting you – a person close to him or her – to be with him or her. To put it another way, the depressed person's desire for isolation and a safe place is not a rejection of you. Paradoxically the depressed person may crave your company at that point, but if being in your company means being in an unsafe, unhealthy place then the depressed person may give signals you interpret as rejection. This is almost certainly not the case. If you respect the safety and sanctity of the depressed person's space the depressed person may actually want you to join him or her there.

Ask 'Is there anything you would like?' The depressed person may be wanting, for example, a cup of coffee but does not want to go to the kitchen (where the kids/in-laws/neighbours/TV etc. are) or simply perceives that the effort involved in making the coffee is too much. Remember, it can be the simple things that count most.

Ask the depressed person if you can sit (lie, lean back, walk ...) with them. This conveys to the depressed person two things. Firstly you recognize that the depressed person has withdrawn into a safe personal space and secondly, you respect that space and as a consequence of that respect you are asking permission to enter that space. This means that the depressed person is in control of his or her environment. The depressed person may not answer, in which case I would interpret their silence as a qualified 'yes'; in other words you are welcome providing you realize that this is my space and you enter it on my terms.

What do you do when you get there?

Here, in my opinion, is the crucial bit. You are not there to counsel the depressed person, to offer advice or to troll through their troubles with them or even for them. You cannot stop the depressed person from being depressed any more than you can stop the sun from shining. You do not need to tell the depressed person this. They already know it. They know you cannot solve their problem for them. They are depressed, not stupid. But you do need to realize it yourself.

So what are you doing there? Having gently and carefully entered the depressed person's safe place, what are you to do there?

Be with them.

The very fact that you are there speaks volumes. Remember that the depressed person craves company to break the isolation, but only company that will not make any demands on him or her and indeed company that will be gently supportive of him or her.

One example of this is a cinematic study of depression entitled *'Melancholia'*, a film by Lars von Trier. The film documents the strained relationship between two sisters, Justine and Claire, as a rogue planet (named Melancholia) bears down on the Earth to bring about the Earth's total destruction. A few words about the film, as the symbolism is not easily interpreted if you have little experience of depression. The rogue (blue) planet Melancholia symbolizes depression, hence its name and colour. The impending destruction that no-one can do anything to avoid indicates the destructiveness that depression can bring about. Justine is the person suffering depression and Claire is the person trying to help her. The film looks at this situation firstly from the point of view of Justine and then from the point of view of Claire. This latter part of the film is particularly relevant to the material we are considering in this chapter.

The best way to be gently supportive is to *be* with someone, that is, to share in their human *being*. (This is relevant to all forms of trauma 'counselling' so to speak, not just depression.)

If you are *being* with someone who is at that time very vulnerable it is important that, to put it bluntly, you have your own shit together. You cannot bring your shit with you when you enter the sacred and safe place of the depressed person. That is why I have indicated above that if you do not have your shit together it is best just to walk away. To repeat what I said above, doing nothing is better than doing harm. (In medical ethics this is called non-maleficence.)

Take a moment to think about this. It is more than just a case of physically being with someone who is depressed. It seeks to capture the essence of what philosophers mean by 'being' (there is even a branch of philosophy devoted to the study of 'being': Ontology). You are *being* with someone, someone who is depressed. From that person's point of view the really important thing is that you are there by *choice*, not by compulsion. In other words, while they may think everyone else has given up on them and while they may even think they have given up on themselves *you have not given up on them.* That, so to speak, is the heart of the matter.

How do you effectively communicate this to the depressed person? There are two things I think it is important to say.

The first is 'I don't want you to die. I want you to live.' But only say it if you mean it. The nature of depression means that depressed people can see through bullshit and pretence much more easily than people who are not depressed. (This invites another, more philosophical question: Are depressed people depressed because they see that much of life is bullshit or does their depression enable them, by discerning what is important and what is not, to see the ubiquitous bullshit?) This cuts right to the heart of the matter. The depressed person is in a position where everything is black. (Recall the line in the Rolling Stones song *'Paint it black'*: 'It's not easy facing up when your whole world is black.') If the depressed person is not actively thinking about suicide then they are more than likely passively thinking about it – it's there as an option, perhaps the only option, and they simply cannot be unaware of this.

By saying this to the depressed person you are effectively addressing the worst case scenario. It is as if you are reaching under the depression and lifting the depressed person out of the depression, at least a little. Remember that one of the drivers of suicide is the thought that the depressed person is of no use to anyone and that no-one would care if they died; in essence, the world would be better off without them. By affirming the positive you are effectively rendering this thinking impotent.

The second thing to say is consequential to the first. Again it seeks to anticipate the depressed person's thinking, which may now go something like this: 'If I am not going to kill myself then I am going to live. If I am going to live what the hell do I do now?' In response to this either spoken or unspoken sentiment you need to reassure the depressed person that 'there is always a way through' any given situation. Specifically, in any situation there is always one response, one course of action that is demonstrated to be rationally superior to any other possible course of action. Note the word 'rationally'. At this stage it is imperative to be rational, to think like a tree diagram which gives the expanse of all rational responses and to choose the one path through the diagram which gives the best response. It means, to labour the point because it is important, to think in terms of 'If I can go from A to B, and if I can go from B to C, then I must be able to go from A to C'.

The effect of such a rational discourse is to immediately clear the field of any irrational thinking, the sought of thinking that is in all probability going round and round inside the depressed person's head. The way forward is now suddenly a lot clearer. The choice has narrowed, the task of living is becoming manageable. (The adoption of rational thinking when I was suicidal is the only reason I am here today.)

So we have said 'I don't want you to die' and 'There is always a way through'. Those are the two important things to say to a depressed person. Isn't there something else? Isn't it obvious the next step is to delineate what that way through is?

Yes and no (the ultimate decisive answer).

Yes because the next step may be simply encouraging the depressed person to eat something, take a shower, have a nap, go to bed, sit with you on the couch and so on. In other words the thing to do next is to attend to immediate needs and comforts. It is quite encouraging, to both the depressed person and the person helping them, how much these simple rational concerns, when met, help the depressed person. Remember that it is sometimes, even often times, the small things that count.

No because in terms of addressing the depressed person's depression and consequent situation they, and in all probability you as the person trying to help them, may not be sure just what that next step is. Indeed you may actually have no idea. But that does not matter. It simply does not matter that you do not know what the next step is. It does not matter you do not know the way through – it is simply enough that you know that there *is* a way through. Remember the black hole analogy - stuff does come out of, or moves through, a black hole, even if we don't know how or why. Finding that way through is something you and the depressed person can do together. It can become something of an adventure, like getting lost in the sand dunes and finding your way back to the beach, or getting off a plane/train/bus/ship in a strange city and finding your way to the place where you will stay. You can do that together. It then becomes part of your *being* with the depressed person.

Being.

The importance of being with a person in distress is poignantly illustrated in the 2016 film '*Fukushima, Mon Amour*' (German title '*Grüsse aus Fukushima*') by German director Doris Dörrie. (In exploring the importance of being Dörrie begins with self-discovery occasioned by significant distress (the Fukushima nuclear incident is only part of it), notes how this could so easily lead to self-destruction (in this case suicide) and celebrates the triumph of being with self-redemption.)

Single cell thingies exist in some primordial type soup somewhere but human beings *be.* Sharing this being with another human being is I think one of the most intimate things that human beings can do. Such sharing is then an anathema to depression and everything it represents. It is one of the most profound things we human beings do, but it does require a lot of reflection, a lot of self-knowledge and a lot of risk. Discovering one's being and being with another human being on their journey of discovery is not for the faint hearted. Such self-discovery has the possibility of becoming self-destructive, something the depressed person knows only too well. But you, the person trying to help the depressed person, must know that self-discovery can also be self-redeeming[11].

Now we have gotten to the heart of the matter. It is pointless trying to reverse depression, trying to undo it, pretend it isn't there or pretend that it was there but now it is 'cured'. (I cringe every time I hear people (politicians are the worst) talking about depression being 'cured'.) To

---

[11] The ideas of self-destruction and self-redemption in relation to self-discovery are explored by the German writer Christa Wolf in her novel *'City of Angels',* particularly around p. 205 in the first American edition (pub. 2013).

put this another way, once a person starts on the road to depression it is pointless trying to get them to turn around, go back or somehow retrace their steps in order to pretend the depression simply is not happening. (This was what was expected of me in the first few years of my depression and because I did not know any better I thought this was the way to go. Needless to say it was not and it simply resulted in another meltdown.) The depression returns again, perhaps even more severe this time. Now the depressed person is back to square one and nothing of any consequence has been achieved in regard to his or her depression.

The point then is to see it through.

In my mind 'seeing it through' means getting to a point where the depressed person is able to manage their depression fairly well on their own with low level support being available. To reiterate what I have already said it is to get to a point where the depressed person has the depression, rather than the depression having the depressed person. In other words, the depressed person is more in control of their depression than the depression is in control of them.

So this is the aim. But how do we help someone get there? How do we help them see it through? To answer this question I am going to draw on what may seem to some an unlikely source: the *Book of Job* in the Hebrew Scriptures. Now before you think I really have lost it this time and am about to fly off on a Bible –quoting rant let me assure you nothing is further from the truth.

The *Book of Job* was written (best guess) around the sixth century BCE, at a time when similar themed writings existed in Egypt and in what was then called Mesopotamia. The book seeks to answer one important question: If God is all-powerful and God is good and compassionate, then why do the righteous suffer? To this end it is as much to do with theology as with the endurance of the human spirit. It is the latter we will focus on for it is there that we find relevance to depression. This relevance lies in the attitude and mindset of Job as a whole series of tribulations are foisted upon him by an omnipotent god who seems to delight in testing the resolve of his worshippers.

An aside. I just cannot let the idea of an omnipotent god go unchallenged, at least because the depressed person may, if the idea of an omnipotent god is championed, inadvertently come to the conclusion that their depression is a punishment of some kind from this god and therefore there is little they can do about it, apart from feel worse than they already feel.

The problem for believers in a divine omnipotent, just and compassionate god is why, if God is so powerful and so just and so compassionate, do bad things happen to good people? No robust theological solution to this problem has ever been presented, no matter what the fundamentalists say. I am of the opinion that no answer has been presented because there is simply no answer to present. The reasoning is quite simple: if God is just and compassionate then God cannot be omnipotent, for such a God would surely not allow bad things to happen to good people, yet they do. If God is omnipotent and just then God cannot be compassionate, yet compassion is one of the core natures of just about any religion you can name.

So, out of omnipotence, justice and compassion, you can have two, but not all three. They are logically incompatible. The one that falls off in philosophical thought is the omnipotence of God. God is simply not all powerful. (God as a separate objective divine entity *not existing* may well have a lot to do with this. Indeed the Good Lord probably really appreciates not existing if doing so means putting up with the religious people around today.)

Consequently we are not much concerned with the theological reflections in the *Book of Job*, which we may loosely categorize as 'God talk'. We will, in any case, advance a 'replacement' if you will for the causal activity of our non-existent divine being in the next chapter, a chapter that will seek to explain *why* we should encourage others to do as Job did to help them cope with depression.

Job's response to the many troubles sent his way was simple. He did not rant and rail at the injustice of it all. He did not wonder what he had done to deserve such treatment. He did not hide in a corner gradually becoming a shadow of the man he once was. So what did he do?

He endured.

It is that simple.

To put it another way he hung in there. His faith in his god, a faith we might interpret in our age as a faith in the goodness of life, never wavered. (Rather than think of Job was some great devout man from long ago the likes of which the world just does not see any more let us remember that the story of Job is just that, a story, and it is told at least in part to reinforce the advantage of faith in this goodness.) That is, he didn't chuck in his towel, bugger off to the desert or drown his sorrows in cheap alcohol, tempting though the latter option may be. He endured.

So how do you encourage a depressed person to endure what they are going through?

The first thing to do is to get the depressed person to accept that if they do not know what to do then the best thing is to do nothing. Deciding to do nothing is a decision and it is quite different from *not* deciding anything. Doing nothing is better than doing something that makes things worse, such as suicide. If it appears to you that the depressed person is choosing between doing nothing and suicide, doing nothing wins out every time. (This is where you can insert the 'I want you to live' intervention.)

The thing about doing nothing is that while the depressed person is doing it time passes and as time passes things invariably change. (There is a scientific theory in support of this that we will explore in the next chapter.) As things change options change. Focus on the rational options, as I have previously mentioned. In any situation there is one rational way forward, one rational thing to do which is the best thing to do in that situation. It may not be a big thing, it may not be a hard thing to do, but it is a rational thing, it is within the capability of the depressed person to do it and having done it the depressed person will have at least a glimmer of a sense of accomplishment. It may be, as I have previously said, something as simple as having a shower and putting on clean clothes. (In the depths of depression, this seemingly innocuous everyday task can present as a huge challenge.)

That thing is done. What, then, is the next rational thing to do? And so on, and so on, until a whole series of simple rational tasks or activities lead the depressed person to realize that they are in fact carrying on with this messy and uncertain business we call living. (For the mathematically inclined philosopher (or the philosophically inclined mathematician) this is known as an inductive approach. That is, if in a series determined by $f(x)$ (that we might call life) you can determine $f(x_n)$, the nth term (in our analogy, the rational thing to do) and then determine $f(x_{n+1})$, the next term in the series (in our analogy, the next rational thing to do) then you have determined the whole series $f(x)$ (in our analogy, the business of living). The alternative to an inductive approach is a deductive approach, which seeks to know, or solve, everything all at once. This is another reason why the idea of an omnipotent god just will not fly. It seeks to impose a deductive solution on an inductive system. This is another way of saying that life is more subjective than objective.)

Nothing breeds success like success. The idea is that the depressed person gradually develops a history of positive achievement. Empowered by this experience the depressed person carries on to achieve even more. It is exactly the same idea that you encounter when tramping (what the Americans call 'hiking') up the side of a steep valley. After a time you are very tired and the top of the valley is nowhere in sight. You come to a place where you can look back and see how far you have come, how far above the valley floor you are. Reflecting on how far you have come gives you the encouragement to carry on. (Yes, I am speaking from experience, and my pack was quite heavy because I was carrying all the booze.)

What I have tried to paint here is a picture of how someone close to a depressed person might go about helping that person. If you are the helper, know your task is not an easy one. Walking on eggshells is generally a lot easier than trying to navigate your way through someone else's depression. I have tried to outline attitudes and approaches that I have found useful, either through direct experience or through intellectual reflection. I cannot, as I have said before, simply say 'Do this' and the depressed person will instantly be no longer depressed.

This leads to my final encouragement to the helper, to the person being with the depressed person. It is simply this: be prepared for a long haul. Learning to manage and cope with depression takes time and energy and money; but mostly time and energy. Time for the depressed person is measured in years, not months or weeks, and does not conform to any therapeutic guidelines some organization or health professional may bandy about. It is a long haul. So as the depressed person is encouraged to endure, so too are you the helper. Hang in there. Things will change. In the next chapter we will see why.

## 7.  The Chaos of Depression.

Chaos and depression may seem like unlikely companions for each other. Mentioning one in the same sentence as the other may remind you of the chaos that evolves in the wake of the depressed person's disinclination to do anything. Dishes not done, beds not made, clothes (and bodies) not washed, lawns not mown and gardens not weeded all carry the hallmarks of the depressed person, the more so the more of them that appear coincidently. But this is not what I mean when I talk about chaos and depression.

So what do I mean? And how does this relate to the idea of endurance postulated at the end of the last chapter?

What I mean is Chaos Theory. Yes, there is a theory called Chaos Theory and it does seem to apply to a lot of what constitutes life, including the 'life' of the planet, if the planet can be considered as a whole (think of the Gaia hypothesis).

Let's look at it this way.

Towards the end of the last chapter I promoted the desirability of thinking rationally when trying to haul yourself or help someone else out of the depths of depression. Think of the next rational thing to do and then the next rational thing after that. I know this works when it seems to you that the only 'choice' you have in front of you is suicide simply because it has worked for me. It works in a crisis. (Emergency service workers adopt the same approach when arriving at the scene of an emergency, say a car crash. You do not see paramedics running around in a panic despite the horrors they may have to deal with. Rather, they work quietly, efficiently and rationally in the face of what most of us would regard as a horrible situation.)

But life is not all rational. Sometimes things happen out of the blue, so to speak. Had the February 2011 Christchurch earthquake occurred a few days earlier, when I spent most of the day in central Christchurch, I could easily have been among the casualties. Sometimes you are just in the wrong place at the wrong time.

At the same time as we realize that things just happen, we know that it is not always the case. The Christchurch earthquake occurred, literally, at a moment in time. For many years prior to this event and for the years following this event many thousands of people have been in central

Christchurch and they were not casualties of an earthquake.

I must relate a story here which would seem to have little to do with depression, but the compulsion to relate this story is almost overwhelming. The Sunday after the September 2010 earthquake the Christchurch Cathedral congregation was thankful that their cathedral had emerged largely unscathed from the earthquake. At that Sunday service the Christchurch Cathedral Theologian (yes there is, or was, such a post) preached that 'God has spared our cathedral and us' or words to that effect.

After the February 2011 earthquake the Christchurch Cathedral was a mess, its spire having toppled into the body of the cathedral, its front end exposed to the weather and its sides showing signs of significant movement. I notice that the same person, the Cathedral Theologian, did not stand in the rubble of the ruined cathedral and preach the same message. Presumably the conclusion must have been reached that God was pissed off at the congregation because this time He (in such instances, God is always a 'He') did not save the Cathedral from the ravages of the earthquake.

The rub here, apart from my little theological rant, is that there is no one causal agent behind such things as earthquakes or illnesses or accidents. We can trace causality back, in the case of earthquakes, to tectonic plates and a liquid core so that we can explain to some extent why these things happen. But there is not someone or something willing these things to happen.

The same is true with the remarkable complexity of life (in every sense of the word) on the planet, and indeed in the universe and of the universe itself (and any other universes that we do not yet know of). Such complexity is not the result of a single causal agent, what we often like to call a 'designer'. Quite simply a design does *not* need a designer. Think Darwin.

In relation to depression (getting back on task) we can conclude that depression is not someone's fault, no-one intended us or anyone else to have depression and the world is not conspiring against us.

So life is not always rational, neither is it always irrational. So what is it? It would seem to be somewhere between being wholly rational and wholly irrational (Aristotle's doctrine of the mean makes another appearance). This somewhere in between is called chaotic, or chaos theory.

Another way to look at the same thing is to think about the chances of something happening. Let us say that you do a regular commute to and from work, by car. How long will it take you to drive home from work tomorrow (or the next working day if tomorrow is not a working day)? You may answer about half an hour, because that is what it usually takes. Then I ask, what is the probability your commute will take less than twenty-five minutes? You might answer, about 30 per cent. On a good day when the traffic is not too bad you can accomplish your commute in twenty-five minutes.

Now, what is the probability your commute will take less than thirty-five minutes? This is the situation on most days but you recognize that if the traffic is heavy and the weather bad your commute can take longer than thirty-five minutes. So you answer, about eighty percent. The longer time you set aside for your commute the higher the probability of doing the commute within that time. This seems quite straight forward.

Now what is the probability your commute will take less than one hour? It is tempting to say, one hundred percent. An event with a probability of one hundred percent is certain to occur. When you set off from work to drive home it means that you will *certainly* arrive home in less than an hour. But can you say that will be the case?

No. It is highly probable that indeed you will arrive home in less than one hour, say something like ninety-eight percent probability. But not certain. Why?

You may be delayed by a flat tyre or a traffic accident. You may even be involved in a traffic accident. There may be a large earthquake that renders the roads impassable. (Yes, this is extremely unlikely, but as the people of Christchurch will tell you, it does happen.) You may suffer a medical incident on the way home. There are all sorts of things that might intervene to prevent you getting home in less than one hour. The probability that any of these will happen on any particular commute is small but it is a probability all the same. The only time you can be one hundred percent certain that you will accomplish your commute within one hour is when you pull into the driveway of your home less than an hour since leaving work.

In a sense that is the simple essence of chaos theory. We cannot say that something will definitely happen and we cannot say that something will definitely not happen. All we can do is speculate about the probability of it happening. (Probability is also the hallmark of the quantum mechanics developed by the German physicist Max Planck in the 1930's.)

This removal of certitude is what gives chaos theory its name. In this sense the term chaos is quite specific. It indicates something that simply cannot be predicted with certainty. Too put it another way every prediction is qualified by a relevant probability.

The lack of the ability to predict what comes next is one of the accepted hallmarks of a chaotic system.

Another is that the system is generated by an iterative function. Put simply, that means that the $n^{th}$ term in a series will be used to determine the $(n+1)^{th}$ term. In terms of human being, it is saying that where you are now will help determine where you will be tomorrow. In technical literature this is referred to as the deterministic aspect of the chaotic system, meaning that the nature of such determinism will yield a unique evolution. The chaotic system thus determined is non-linear; that means if it was graphed (presented as a picture) it would not be a straight line.

The third hallmark of a chaotic system is its sensitivity to initial conditions. This means that how it starts out has a huge bearing on which way it evolves. (There is no one accepted definition of chaos theory but what I have reported here seems to me to be the guts of the matter.)

The application of uncertainty to the human condition, particularly the iterative nature of chaos theory and its sensitivity to initial conditions, is explored in the 2012 film *'Cloud Atlas'*, directed by Tom Tykwer and Lana Wachowski.

By way of another example let me report the 'discovery' (or, perhaps more correctly, the re-discovery) of chaos theory.

A meteorologist by the name of Edward Lorenz was using mathematical equations to predict weather patterns. Initially he used input data accurate to six decimal places, and in using this data got a certain result. For economy, he then inputted the same data but this time accurate to only three decimal places, expecting essentially the same result as before. To his surprise the effect of rounding off his data to three decimal places generated a completely different result from the same data inputted with six decimal places. (The idea here is that rounding off produces an inaccuracy. For example 0.005 includes any number between 0.0045 and 0.0054999... as both of these numbers, when rounded to three decimal places, give

0.005.) This illustrates a sensitivity to initial conditions (in this case the input data) that Lorenz was simply unaware of.

Lorenz famously described this sensitivity by suggesting that a butterfly flapping its wings in the Amazon could, six months later, produce a large storm over the mainland United States. This sensitivity to initial conditions is thus known as the 'butterfly effect'.

The effect has been explored in a number of films, for example the 1998 film '*Sliding Doors*' directed by Peter Howitt, where there are two plots.

In the first plot the lead character rushes down the stairs of the tube station and manages to catch the (London) tube train just as the doors slide closed behind her. This gives rise to one plot which proceeds with particular flow on consequences.

In the second plot she is just a fraction of a second late and the doors slide closed in front of her, meaning she has missed that particular tube train. This naturally gives rise to flow on consequences, but consequences that are quite different from the first plot.

So what has all this got to do with depression?

Let's go through the three descriptors or hallmarks of chaos theory and see how they relate to depression. To be awkward, or difficult or just plain onerous we will consider these descriptors in reverse order.

Let's consider the idea of sensitivity to initial conditions or the butterfly effect as it is popularly known. We can sum this up in another way which begins to find relevance to dealing with depression, yours or someone else's. Small things matter. That's it. Simple as that.

When we look at the quality of our lives, regardless of whether we are experiencing depression (either directly or indirectly through being close to someone with depression), we note, and we are told in countless health and well-being columns, that it is the small things that matter. There are, in my view, two main reasons for this.

Firstly, in our routine lives it is the small things that tend to add quality to our lives. This could be because it is the small things we have most control over or because we value the quality those small things bring to our lives as icing on the cake as it were. It is, in all probability, a mixture of both. So we feel as if a humdrum routine afternoon has been qualified by a courteous gesture of another, an act of consideration that goes beyond what we might normally expect or a random act of kindness. Anything that makes us feel we are human beings who actually live Life, and are not just biological functionaries whose only purpose is the exercise of some sort of utility, adds to our well-being, our sense of who we are rather than what we do.

Secondly, as our lives are qualified by such consideration we feel a greater motivation to extend the same consideration to others, thus qualifying their lives. The example often given in this context is that of smiling at a person on the street. You will probably not see that person again that day, maybe even that week or (in a big city) ever again. Consequently you will never know the effect your smile had on that person. Such positive considerations spread like a contagion.

If your consideration is extended to a depressed person (how would you know, you ask, to which I would reply, how would you *not* know) you may have just done a whole lot more for that person than you realize. If you *are* the depressed person, then know that you have done a good thing for someone else, *which means that you are also capable of doing a good thing for yourself.*

Another application of chaos theory to depression is to relate how dependent we all are on the genes we have inherited from our parents and thus from other (dubious) ancestors. These are the initial conditions we are born with and we cannot do a damn thing about them, apart from possibly being aware of them. One could also argue with some validity that the influence of these initial conditions also extends into our formative years. I have said previously that my depression is rooted in a childhood environment which, by the time I became aware of it, I could do nothing about. By the time we figure out quite what we are born with and quite what our formative environment was like, it is far too late to change either of these things. To put it in the popular and somewhat blunt expression, we can choose our friends but we cannot choose our family.

In other words our tendency to suffer from depression may stem from our own initial conditions, that is, it may be something we are born with, and, or, may be the result of what happened to us in our formative years. These unique initial conditions and our sensitivity to them are why two people may suffer the same trauma and yet each person will have a different response to that trauma. Our timelines of life are as unique as we are. For this reason, the idea that 'I coped with all this stuff and so you should be able to do the same' is simply not valid. Because of our unique initial conditions we all have differing reactions to what may seem to be the same events. The message here is simple; if you have a tendency to suffer from depression do not beat yourself up about it. In all probability (literally) there is nothing you could have done, or can do, about this, except to deal with it.

The second hallmark of chaos theory is the thing about it being an iterative function. Basically, as I have said previously, this means that the term of the function $f(x)$ you have now (usually called the $n^{th}$ term) is what is used to work out the next term of the function (usually called the $(n+1)^{th}$ term). Then the $(n+1)^{th}$ term becomes the $n^{th}$ term and is used to determine the next $(n+1)^{th}$ term. And so we progress, term by term, through the function in an iterative fashion. This may sound very technical but it is not.

Consider walking. When we walk we put one foot in front of the other. Because we only have two feet, which foot is the one that goes in front and which foot is the one behind us alternates. But the foot that goes in front can only do so if the foot behind us is on solid ground. When the foot that goes in front finds solid ground it quickly becomes the foot behind us as the foot behind now becomes the foot in front, searching out more solid ground. And so, step by step, we can actually cover vast distances by simply taking one step at a time.

This is so obvious in our normal everyday life we are often not consciously aware of what we doing. We become more aware of what we are doing when the ground we walk over is challenging and greater concentration is needed. Consider a bunch of school kids making their way along a mountain stream, no doubt on a school camp. They have to cross this stream to get to where they are going. The stream is hewn with large boulders, which are both an impediment to progress and a means of making progress.

The kids who look at the stream and the boulders hewn about its channel and then look at the smooth ground on the other side, which they are aiming to reach, will in all probability freeze, impeded by the barrier presented by the boulders in front of them. They are looking at the thing as one impassable whole and are thus daunted by it.

The kids who simply look where they will place their next step, on this boulder or that boulder, ensuring each step is secure before bringing the back foot to the front to search for the next step, will be across the stream in no time. I have observed kids doing this and you can see the look of concentration on their faces as they simply progress from one boulder, one secure foothold, to the next. They are focused on where the next step goes, rather than looking at the barrier of boulders as a whole and being daunted by it.

This is an iterative function at work.

The relevance of all this to depression may now be clear. The depressed person needs to take one day at a time, even one hour at a time. If they can get through the next hour, *then* (and only then) they can concentrate on the one that follows. Trying to solve the whole depression thing at one time is like looking at the stream and seeing a barrier of boulders. It leaves us frozen, unable to function, unable to perceive a way through this barrier. The barrier becomes insurmountable and the depressed person quickly concludes that suicide is the only viable alternative. But simply looking where to place our next step, where to place the foot coming forward, can see us work our way through the barrier, literally step by step.

We can take the application of chaos theory to the management of depression further.

We recall that the hallmarks of a chaotic system, in the order we are now considering them, are that the system is very sensitive to initial conditions, is iterative and that we cannot predict with certainty what comes next.

The human body is one such system.

Sensitivity to initial conditions is illustrated by how our genetic inheritance will determine to some extent our health over the course of our lives. Also, how we start off in life (the first few formative years) determines to a large extent how we go in life.

The state of our bodies at any given time will determine the state of our bodies in the near future; major bodily transformations do happen but (surgery notwithstanding) these still take time and proceed in an iterative fashion.

The third hallmark of chaos theory is illustrated by the fact that none of us knows with any certainty what the state of our body will be in the middle or far future. While we may predict with some degree of certainty what that state will be (that is, with some probability, based on what the state of our bodies is now and has been in the recent past) it is only a probabilistic prediction. Health columns are full of stories of fit and healthy people struck down by disease in the prime of their lives (I am thinking particularly of the sad case of Helen Kelly, President of the Council of Trade Unions in New Zealand at the time of writing, who was diagnosed with incurable lung cancer in her early fifties after feeling a pain 'in her middle' and who has never smoked).

On the other side of the coin this lack of certainty may work in our favour. Former United States president Ronald Reagan famously said in a speech something like 'I have already lived twenty more years than my life expectancy at birth indicated' or something to that effect.

The experience of depression leads us to consider the future as a long dark road devoid of light and hope, down which we must make our way.

But the unpredictability of our chaotic lives leads us to conclude that whatever the future is it will not be just as we think it will be. Yes, bad things happen unexpectedly. But so do good things. We simply do not know what is around the corner. (Hence the philosophical imperative to live for the moment (carpe diem), of which I was reminded of yesterday by my seventy-nine year old neighbour, Mary, who I think is a delightful person.)

So what can we conclude from all this? Rather than focus on the uncertainty of chaos theory, and remember that this uncertainty is a long way from being random, let us focus on the sensitivity to initial conditions indicated by chaos theory and the idea of an iterative progression, also indicated by chaos theory. Perhaps we should pause here to note that chaos theory is itself inductive, or in the jargon of philosophers 'a posteriori', Latin for something like 'after the experience' (posterior – behind). This means that arising out of our human being (the inductive approach) is a sensitivity to initial conditions that (if we now include the probabilistic or uncertainty aspect of chaos theory) suggests if we do some small good thing then this will compound into some bigger good thing, of which we will be unaware of.

Now it sounds familiar. If we inject goodness into life then goodness will manifest in our lives. In what ways, by what means we simply cannot predict. But there is, I suggest, a base realization that this is simply so. All I have done is nut out the mechanics of how this might be so.

And so there is hope. Our hope is built on what we ourselves think and do. Even as I write these words I am conscious of giving myself that message as well as sharing it with others. It is one thing to know that this is so; it is quite another to act on this knowledge.

In order to act on this knowledge our hope must have a context. To simply encourage someone to have hope is in itself self-defeating, for hope as an ideal (like justice) is simply unobtainable. To simply have hope is to wish for something we cannot have. Rather we need to have hope in something, for something. To fulfill that hope we need to do something to make it happen. Hope then is not just a passive pie-in-the-sky thing but a real expectation grounded in our own particular context. For example, any hope I might have of being an Olympic athlete, given my age and arthritis, would be totally unreasonable. But if I hoped for something in which I had some proficiency (say, philosophy) then that hope is not unreasonable. To realize that hope I simply cannot just sit at my desk and expect it to come to fruition. The realization of hope involves hard work and dedication. Finding hope while in the depths of depression is no different.

If all this talk of chaos theory seems a bit much then let me simplify the discourse down to a basic couple of things that I think we can conclude from all this. These conclusions are aimed at the person suffering from depression but are also relevant to the person helping someone suffering from depression.

Firstly, hang in there. This is restating the imperative to endure that we have looked at earlier. Take one day, one hour at a time and take the time to think about where you are going to place your next step, rather than, to use our earlier analogy, trying to figure out how to cross the stream (deal with the depression) in one go. Endure. Be. However you want to phrase it, simply hang in there, remembering that doing nothing is better than doing something that would cause you or someone else harm.

Why? Because, and secondly, things will change. Now it is easy to say that but there is an unspoken qualification here that I think needs to be voiced. It is this: things around you will change, *even if you do not initiate change*. In all probability they will change for the better. We can say this because when you are in an endurance mode you deliberately, and possibly even unconsciously, limit your existence to rational decisions – simple decisions based around the question 'What do I need to do in order to survive?' Thus irrationality is minimized, reduced down to virtually nothing. The things you do will be good things in their own small way and good things encourage other good things to happen.

If that is all you take from this discourse on chaos theory then that is still a good thing.

## 8.    **The nobility of depression.**

The nobility of depression arises, in my mind, from anecdotal observations of people who have battled with depression and people who have witnessed, or been close to, someone who has experienced depression.

Nobility of depression arises from the idea that such people exhibit a nobility which is not found in the general population.

They seem to have, in the eyes of others, a greater sense of self and a greater awareness of what is important in life and, complementarily, what is not important.

Such a sense of self and such an awareness of what is important in life is not, of course, limited to those who have dealt, or are successfully dealing, with depression. I once acquired, as a birthday present, a book of photographs documenting the twentieth century (1999: Bruce Bernard Ed. *'Century'*; Phaidon Press, London) which has on page 671 a 1963 photograph of a Liverpool docker, attributed to Colin Jones, who exhibits what I would call a nobility of the self. The citation accompanying the photograph speaks of 'a man whose self-possession and general demeanour anyone might envy'.

Yet it remains that there seems be at least a correlation between depression and the nobility of the self. We must exercise some care and note that a correlation is just that. It is not necessarily indicative of a cause and effect relationship.

In short, we might say that there is an upside to having depression.

What I want to do is explore what that upside is, how that upside may be useful in this great enterprise we call human endeavour and why there is this upside at all.

In essence we have already suggested what this upside is. It is a greater sense of self and a greater awareness of what is important in life (which may not be the same as what other people, and, or, society, implicitly tell us what is important in life). But what does this mean?

A greater sense of self implies that in some way we can 'sense' the self. In other words we can step outside ourselves and take a look at ourselves and be able to say that the self we are looking at is good. We are reminded of our capacity for second order thought.

In second order thought the self is able to think about what is being, or has been, thought about. In our current context the self is able to take a good look at the self and, hopefully, determine the self to be good. This implies a relationship of the self to the self.[12]

Nobility, when arising from an experience of depression (and, perhaps, in other contexts though these are outside our current parameters of consideration) is then the affirmation that this relationship of the self to the self is good. It is healthy. It is better to have this relationship than not to have it, often, I suspect, much better.

In the context of this relationship the self affirms what is good about the self at the same time as accepting, warts and all, what is not good about the self.

We have a fair understanding of what is not good about the self when that self is afflicted with depression. We know about the withdrawal, the isolation, the lethargy and the frustration that depression occasions. We know how these things manifest themselves in the life of the depressed person. We know about the depressed person's inability to cope with too much of anything, acknowledging their sensitivity to external stimuli is exaggerated. We know about the cognitive effort involved on the part of the depressed person in dealing with his or her depression. We

---

[12] I acknowledge, and am grateful for, the insight of my mental health nurse Donna who talked with me about the importance of the self's relationship to the self.

know about the effort required to think about our selves in something approaching an objective way.

The effort involved in dealing with depression and its consequences also indicates to us the good things about our relationship to ourselves. The pervasiveness of negativity that is depression dominates our self and our perception of our self, mercilessly and unrelentingly negating the very being of that self. But there are good things there behind that negativity. We just need to know, firstly, to look for them and secondly, what to look for when we do look for them.

There is an old idea, the origins of which I do not know but which clearly has evolved from humanity's struggle to be human. We are told, in the midst of our struggle with adversity of whatever form, that what we are going through is 'character building'. The point of this idea is that the realization of our strengths and goodness as human beings often arises out of our experience of adversity.

In this sense, depression is no different to other experiences of adversity. When we look carefully at what is not good about depression we see, hiding behind or under what is not good, some things that are good.

When we think about the depressed person's sensitivity to external stimuli, we usually think about the negative effects of such stimuli. Going to the supermarket is often fraught with overwhelming stimuli for the depressed person, with signs, displays, announcements and choices all competing for the depressed person's attention, and this is before even encountering that group of people who stop right in the middle of the main isle with their fully laden trolleys and talk to someone they have just bumped into. (My particular pet hate is the person you follow through the one way barriers at the supermarket entrance and who then stops dead, entirely ignorant of anyone behind them who might want to get past them, while they decide what it is they actually came for and where they might find it.)

But that same sensitivity can mean the depressed person is an empathetic listener who picks up on the nuances of conversations that other people miss entirely.

That same sensitivity can sense when someone is upset but is desperately trying to hide it to stave off embarrassment.

That same sensitivity can sense when someone is struggling with something (or someone) but does not want to admit this to avoid embarrassment or ridicule, or does not want to appear 'weak' in the eyes of others.

This is because the sensitivity of the depressed person allows that same person to see things as they really are and not as they might be, or even not as someone else intends them to be. There is an existential reality to the world of the depressed person which is not readily available to other people.

To put it another way, the depressed person can spot bullshit from quite a distance. The depressed person then takes little or no countenance of the ubiquitous bullshit[13], leaving the depressed person with a more authentic perception of what is really happening. (A prime example, in my opinion, of the bullshit that can so depress the sensitive person is the world view of Roger Douglas, New Zealand parliamentarian and author of the market oriented economic reforms of the late 1980's. Douglas asserts that 'People will always pursue their own self-interests...'[14].)

---

[13] The prevalence, and necessity, of bullshit in the modern world is indicated in an elegant little book by Harry G Frankfurt, emeritus professor of philosophy at Princeton University, entitled, appropriately, '*On Bullshit*', 2005, Princeton University Press, Princeton.

[14] Roger Douglas in Dean, Andrew; 2015: *Ruth, Roger and Me.* Bridget Williams Books, Wellington; page 58

This leads to what might be called an existential question, one which we have asked before but one which I shall repeat, albeit in a slightly different way: does the depressed person see things as they really are as a result of their depression or does the person who sees things as they really are become depressed as a result of their insight?

In the manner of all either/or questions the likely answer is both. That is, that the depressed person sees things as they really are is both a cause and an effect, one and the other.

This indication of what is important is a positive outcome of one's experience of depression.

It thus enables one to connect empathetically with those whom polite society, and I use the term loosely, would otherwise ride roughshod over. In short, we need such people in our society. We need people who see things as they really are and we need people who, consequently, can empathize with those disaffected by what we usually term polite society. To put it bluntly, there is a good reason why the owl, who sits and watches and sees things others miss, is considered wise.

Such insight, or to continue with the owl thing, such wisdom, is the basis for the depressed person's necessary cognitive efforts if he or she is not to be overcome by depression. The depressed person ruminates about what is really there, as opposed to what they may think is really there, and reaches conclusions based on that rumination. Such thinking, simply because of the process which gives rise to such thinking, is likely, more likely than not, to give rise to greater insight about the human condition.

In other words, we, that is humanity in all its glorious expanse, need people who can sit back, reflect, take stock and express the results of their ruminations. We need people who reflect on the direction humanity is taking and the things it is doing (or not doing) just as the rugby team (I am, after all, a New Zealander) needs the person who watches and reflects and analyses and acts accordingly. I believe they are called 'coaches' though my knowledge of sport is quite limited.

Why is there such a need? The group that we call humanity, which we might consider in microcosm as a rugby team (hardly an accurate representation of humanity, thankfully), is better for meeting such a need. Think of how a rugby team would fair without its coach, yet he (or she) is but one person compared to the fifteen players who take to the field. This suggests, as does the Dunedin Study, that the primal reason for society having people capable of discernment and reflection and analysis is evolutionary. We do not need a lot of these people (the Dunedin Study reckons on about ten percent of the population if my recall is correct) but we *do* need these people.

To put it another way, we need people in our civilized society who may, or do, not actively participate in the day to day running of that society, but who, like the owl, sit on the sidelines and watch and learn and discern. Without such people it is entirely questionable whether our society would remain civilized for very much longer.

So how come our society throws up a mix of personality and character types, of which our reserved, prone to depression, type is but one? The hint is in the assertion that we need these people in our society. That need has driven the evolution of the sensitive empathetic personality type, a type whose sensitivity and empathy contribute positively to our society at the same time as being a type prone to depression *because of* that sensitivity and empathy. Evolution has the knack of delivering just what is needed, simply because living organisms (of which human beings are but one) evolve to suit the environment they are living in. It is a bit like asking why does the water take the shape of the glass when you pour the water into the glass. It is impossible to get the water into the glass without it taking the shape of the glass. Similarly life evolves to have the very attributes necessary for life to evolve.

It is the necessity to society of such sensitive and empathetic people and the minority of such people in the general population which suggests to us nobility.

A further observation is I think relevant.

Dealing with depression is also much more about who we are than what we do. Put bluntly, it is more about being than doing. In human society we tend to think more about doing than being. (Think about the highly unoriginal question people, and especially men, are asked at social occasions: 'What do you do?')

Being rather than doing is something of a double-edged sword.

In the nascent nation of New Zealand being seen to make a contribution to the growth of the nation is important. Thus building highway bridges (what I used to do) is seen as much more relevant and constructive than sitting around thinking about metaphysics (what I do now). Doing more often than not trumps being in New Zealand society, and, I would suggest, in western societies generally.

As we have seen depression invites, even forces, us to think about what is important in life and particularly in our lives. Whether the depressed person likes it or not, to deal with their depression means self-reflection and self-care, a level of introversion and consideration of *who* you are that necessarily has to trump any consideration of *what* you do. To fail to do this consigns the depressed person to a stagnant existence at the mercy of their depression.

To do this properly is a big ask in itself. Yet people do deal with their depression and they do so by consideration of their being. Think of the self's relationship to the self. This has more to do with being rather than doing.

Is dealing with your depression against overwhelming odds, that is, emphasizing being rather than doing while all around you the reverse is true, an indicator of nobility?

Yes and no. (Never expect a straight answer from a philosopher.)

Yes, because in overcoming any obstacle or barrier, in dealing with adversity of any kind or origin, a high degree of self knowledge and self awareness is generated, often by way of what we might call philosophical reflection, and this is the basis of nobility, at least as I see it.

The nature of depression, as a disease of the same mind which is doing the reflection and exploring the idea of self, would then seem to add an extra impetus to the emergence of a nobility of some sort in a person who is dealing with their depression.

Before we embark on an elitist view of depression and nobility we need to consider some harsh truths. Dealing with depression encompasses a range of therapeutical initiatives that are not limited to the individual and, consequently, do not suggest the nobility of just the individual.

Most, even perhaps all, people enlist outside help to varying degrees in dealing with depression. For some this means that the quality of their lives is mitigated by charitable trusts and welfare agencies, providing sheltered accommodation and help with day to day living.

It is wrong to admonish these people, to say they could do more, or to say that if only they did this or that, or (worse) did what I did, then things would get better. The diversity of human being reminds us that we do not all start on a level playing field and further that the journey thus started is unique for each one of us.

It is entirely right that such lives should be mitigated by society through charity and welfare, for such mitigation says more about those doing the mitigating than those whose lives are mitigated. In this sense there is, in my opinion, nobility attached to such mitigation just as there is nobility attached to any society which looks after those who cannot look after themselves.

No, because nobility can be involved in any human struggle to overcome adversity, even, or especially, if that adversity is not viewed as a consequence of any action on the part of the afflicted person. (The previously mentioned example of Job in the Hebrew Scriptures is again relevant.) Many illnesses and diseases occur independently of any action or activity of the person who has the illness or disease. We have long moved past the point where we blamed sin for illness.

In this sense nobility comes from dealing with adversity that we did not bring on ourselves, that we do not deserve and the effects of which we cannot help. We again acknowledge that people deal with such adversity differently and with different results. Again nobility is found in the attitudes and actions of a compassionate society which mitigates the effects of such adversity on people.

In this sense nobility is not then occasioned solely by dealing with depression. It can arise out of a person's dealing with adversity of any sort and can often arise when ordinary people are forced to deal with extra-ordinary situations. The experience of war (for example, both the First and the Second World Wars) was for many New Zealanders one such situation.

Another example of this, in my view, is Bernie Monk, the spokesperson for the Pike River mining families following the death of twenty-nine miners in 2010 on the West Coast of the South Island of New Zealand in what has since been shown to have been a preventable accident.

But there is still, I think, something about depression which sets it apart from other adverse events and situations. I suspect it has something to do with a point I have alluded to briefly above but now want to consider a little more carefully.

In depression the mind that suffers is also the mind that has to cope with the suffering. To try and cope with this suffering, to mitigate it where possible, is to try and overcome (a glimpse of Nietzschean philosophy here) the mind's depressive imperative to *not* cope with it.

How is such 'overcoming' accomplished? I have previously suggested rational thought has a big part to play here and it is the struggle to establish a rational thought process that I think is part of the key to this overcoming. But something else also plays a part.

I recently saw the latest Mad Max movie *'Fury Road'*. I admit to being something of a petrol head and a sucker for good special effects (in which I wasn't disappointed, which was just as well as the plot wasn't up to much). The vehicles used in the movie all had one thing in common: they were functional. They were not built for comfort, or for looks but solely to serve the purpose they were intended for, be it gun wagons or a mobile music blaster. They had been stripped down and the only additional bits, scavenged from other vehicles, were bits that added to their functionality.

When a person tries to deal with depression they have to do the same thing. Life has to be stripped down to its bare essentials and questions like 'How will I get food?' and 'Where will I sleep?' become important. This is where rationality plays an important part, just as functionality played an important part in the evolution of the vehicles in Mad Max. All unnecessary concerns have to be pushed aside. Life is reduced to bare framework which holds a few essential bits together.

Seeing your life in this (figurative) way leads to realizations and conclusions about what is important in your life. Things you may have hung on to because you thought they somehow contributed to your humanity, such as persevering with a toxic relationship (as I did), are now shown to be not so important after all, and letting go of them may in fact be therapeutic. On the other hand, things that you may have thought of as not so important and thus of little consequence may now, in these changed circumstances, assume a much greater significance in and to your life. These things may be physical things and they may also be things like relationships which need to be encouraged because they are actually more significant than you had realized.

Knowing what is important in life and in particular in your life (such knowing necessarily encompasses its complement – knowing what is *not* important) is part of any significant development of the self. Knowing what is important to you is one of the myriad ways in which you learn to know yourself, or in other words to get to know who you really are. Encouraging this relationship with yourself is, I suggest, a foundation, even a definition, for nobility. The noble self is the self who relates well to itself.

If this idea of relating to yourself sounds a little weird (shades of 'I'm okay and so am I') it is because it is a thing uncommonly done, let alone done well. It requires the second order thinking (thinking about what you are thinking about; fostering the ability to look as objectively as you can at yourself) I have previously mentioned as helpful in a cognitive approach to dealing with depression.

If there is nobility available to those who deal with depression then I think its genesis lies primarily in this relationship with yourself. Such relationships are, in a 'doing' oriented society, rare.

Thus one overcomes the babble of (often conflicting) messages the self receives from the world (society, environment, everything out there so to speak), not only denying those messages the validity they so often fraudulently seek but replacing them with messages (thoughts) which have gestated in your self. The relationship with one's self lies in the articulation of those authentic messages beginning in one's self to one's self. This is a noble thing.

Yet it is a nobility that cannot be claimed. It can only come as a product of life experience and reflection on that experience. Therefore it is not in itself an object to be aimed for or to strive after. It is in the end a nobility of the self; that is all and that is sufficient.

www.ingramcontent.com/pod-product-compliance
Lightning Source LLC
Chambersburg PA
CBHW070809280726
48660CB00015B/89